Learning To Trust
God's Faithfulness

Learning To Trust God's Faithfulness

by
Jeanne Caldwell

Harrison House
Tulsa, Oklahoma

Unless otherwise indicated, all Scripture quotations are taken from the *King James Version* of the Bible.

Learning To Trust God's Faithfulness
ISBN 0-89274-929-6
Copyright © 1995 by Jeanne Caldwell
Agape Church
P. O. Box 22007
Little Rock, AR 72221

Published by Harrison House, Inc.
P. O. Box 35035
Tulsa, OK 74153

Dedication

To the two most loved and important men in my life next to
Jesus: my husband, Happy, and my son, Ronnie.

Contents

Foreword   11

Preface   13

1   But Father. . .I'm a Second-Hand Anna   15

2   Don't Weep For Me, I'm Not Dead. I'm Alive!   19

3   My Child, What Do You Want of Me?   23

4   Dear Lord, Would You Fill My Cup 'Til It Overflows   27

5   You Two Are Just Out On a Lark   31

6   Peace in the Time of Trouble   35

7   I Love You, God...   41

8   God, Why Did You Let That Happen?   45

9   Lord, Are We On The Right Track?   49

10   Use Your Own Faith   53

11   Our Righteousness Is As Filthy Rags   57

12   What Is Your Sign?   61

13   Holy Spirit, I Want To Know You   65

14 Keep Your Eyes On Me and You'll Make It   69

15 What About Me, Lord?   73

16 I Grew Up In A Singing Family   77

17 Receive the Anointing   81

18 A Respecter of the Poor   85

19 His Plan For You   89

20 The Best Years of Our Lives   93

21 The Church as a Whole   97

22 Eruption, Destruction, or Construction?   101

23 No Way   105

24 Peace and Joy — The Choice Is Yours   109

25 It's a Small World   113

26 Thank You, Lord, For My New Kirby   117

27 My People Need To Laugh   121

28 Contentment   125

29 Put The Blame Where It Belongs   129

30 Take Heed To My Ways   133

31 My Mother — A Precious Jewel   137

32 Who Will Pray?   143

33 Hold Fast To Your Dreams   147

34 Baptized Unto Him   151

Foreword

In this book on the subject of God's faithfulness, Jeanne takes real-life encounters with God from her childhood to the present and shares them with you to increase your faith and trust in a loving God.

You can personally relate to Jeanne's simple but profound way of sharing her heart. As her husband, I have seen her walk through most of these experiences. We have walked through some of them together.

Jeanne has a faith that works. She says the reason her faith works is because she loves God — faith works by love.

This book on God's faithfulness will be one that you cannot put down until you have read it through. I guarantee you will be blessed.

Happy Caldwell

Preface

The Lord spoke to me in October of 1983 and asked me to teach a ladies Bible study at Agape Church. After praying and trying to talk God out of it, I said, "Lord, what can I teach these ladies? Some of them are much better equipped to teach than I am. I'd just rather sing."

He said, "I want you to teach the ladies to be mature Christians, to be refined and perfected in every area of life. Just share with them the things I have taught you through the Word that have helped you become victorious."

The Lord confirmed His Word to me through Rev. Charles Rogers of Fort Worth, Texas, whom I had not seen or talked with in years. He called me long distance the night before I was to teach and spoke almost the same exact words. I appreciated the confirmation.

A few years later, I began writing articles called "God's Faithfulness" for the *Agape Newsletter.* Once again, I wanted to help people by sharing very simply and honestly my life-changing experiences with the Lord. Many times people have asked for permission to make copies of the articles to send to others. We have also sent copies of certain articles to help people in situations similar to my own.

Then in September of 1986, Dr. T.L. Osborn gave me this word when he was at our church. He knew nothing about my articles or teaching, but had only seen me minister in song.

"You may not be as eloquent as others, or have detailed outlines like others, but God has marked you to minister what good things He has done in your life...where He has brought you from. Just as He has moved upon you in the singing ministry, He will move upon you in the teaching ministry, with a great anointing and you will have an effect on people. You will affect people when you minister."

The Lord has now prompted me to put these articles in a book and make them available to those who do not receive our newsletter. So, in obedience to Him, I pray this book will bless and inspire you to find out for yourself that God is faithful to His Word and that you can trust Him!

The chapters are not in any certain order as to date or time, but as the Holy Spirit directed me to write them.

Jeanne Caldwell

Chapter One

BUT FATHER...I'M A SECOND-HAND ANNA

Let them shout for joy, and be glad, that favor my righteous cause: yea, let them say continually, Let the Lord be magnified, which hath pleasure in the prosperity of his servant.

Psalm 35:27

In 1974 I went to England, Arkansas, with some ladies in my church to hear a young lady named Carolyn Savelle speak at a women's luncheon. I had heard a lot about the Savelles and was really looking forward to hearing what she had to say.

I don't remember her topic, but I do remember a statement she made that completely changed my life and my way of thinking. She told a story about taking her girls to school and hearing a song on the radio called, "I'm a Second-hand Anna Wearing Second-hand Clothes." She said they all started singing that little tune every time they got in the car to go somewhere. One day Carolyn said suddenly, "Girls, we can't sing that song anymore. We can't say those words out of our mouths, for we will have what we say. We aren't second-

15

hand Annas, wearing second-hand clothes. We are children of the King and His blessings are ours."

When she said that, I felt like someone had hit me in the pit of my stomach. I felt grieved inside because everything I had on had been given to me. In fact, Happy and I had not bought anything for ourselves in the last two years. Every dime went into the ministry. Those of you who are in the ministry know what I am talking about. At any rate, I didn't hear another word she said. That one statement kept going over and over in my head and in my heart. I felt so heavy-hearted.

While driving home, the ladies chatted about what a wonderful meeting it had been and all I could think about were my *second-hand clothes*. When I got home, I went into our bedroom and got down on my knees beside our bed and prayed, "Father, I know that you love me as much as you love Carolyn Savelle, for the Word says that you are no respecter of persons. *But Father, I'm a second-hand Anna, because I wear second-hand clothes.* I don't know how on earth you will do it, but I'm asking you to give me a new dress — one with tags on it!" It was very difficult for me to ask God for a new dress. With all the needs of the ministry, it seemed selfish of me. I didn't know that it would give Him pleasure to give me the desires of my heart and meet the needs of the ministry too! After praying, I got up and thought about it no more.

A week or so passed and Peggy Capps, also from England, Arkansas, called and asked if I would come and sing and share my testimony with her ladies Bible study. I did, and after the meeting she gave me an offering. I was so surprised and blessed. As I was walking to my car, she said to me, "Have you ever been to my daughter's new dress shop?" I said, "No, but I would like to some day." She said, "Well, why don't you drop by on your way home?" I told her I would, then mumbled to myself all the way over there, thinking, "How do I get myself into these messes? I don't have the money to buy anything. I don't know how much my offering was, and I sure don't want to spend it on clothes for myself."

I got to the store and started looking at the clothes. They were so beautiful! Peggy held up a dress and said, "This looks like it would fit you. Why don't you try it on?" I did and it fit. Then I thought, "Now how am I going to get out of buying this dress?" I walked out of the dressing room and she said, "Oh, it fits you perfectly. The Lord wants you to have it." I said, "What do you mean?" (That was the first time anyone had ever said anything like that to me and I was not sure I understood what she meant by "have it.")

She said, "From time to time, we sow seed and give someone a dress so that our business will prosper. I want to give you this dress as *seed.*" I was so elated and surprised. As I was driving home the Lord said to me, "Jeanne, you have a new dress." I said, "Oh, Lord, I know it and I thank You so much. You are so faithful to Your Word!" Then He added, "...with tags on it."

Since that day, I wear second-hand clothes as well as new clothes. I'm just not in bondage to either. I found out that it is God's will to bless and prosper me *and* give me the desires of my heart.

If you don't know that it is God's will to bless you, you will not go to Him in faith, and you will miss many of the blessings He has for you and *wants* to give you. Just remember, the Word works for everyone who believes and stands on it. God doesn't love me anymore than He loves you. So ask, believe, and receive — that your joy may be full!

Chapter Two

DON'T WEEP FOR ME, I'M NOT DEAD. I'M ALIVE!

Saying with a loud voice, Worthy is the Lamb that was slain to receive power, and riches, and wisdom, and strength, and honour, and glory, and blessing.

Revelation 5:12

The Easter season always brings to remembrance something the Lord said to me that totally changed my way of thinking about Calvary.

When I was growing up, I went to all the movies about the Bible and the life of Jesus. During the scenes where He was crucified, I would just cry and cry. Everybody did! It hurt to see Jesus suffer so terribly under the hands of an unthankful, unholy, wicked people. I would actually grieve after the movies were over, as if He were still dead.

One day I was watching a movie called "The Life of Jesus" on KVTN, Channel 25, our new Christian television station in Little Rock. It was produced to minister to heathen people who worship other gods. I have heard that when these people see the film of how Jesus suffered and died as a *man* for them, they are saved by the hundreds.

Their faces actually show the compassion they are experiencing as they see Him suffer. Even my husband, Happy, when he was first saved, wrote a song called, "The Pain He Suffered Was Real." So it is a natural human emotion to weep when we see what Jesus did for us. It actually causes people to come to Christ by the thousands.

One night many years ago, after watching "Jesus of Nazareth," I went to my room to cry over what the Lord had done for me. As I was crying and telling Him how sorry I was that He had to suffer so much and die for me, He interrupted me and said, *"Don't weep for me. I'm not dead. I'm alive."* I was startled at His statement and shocked that He wasn't pleased with my act of love and appreciation for Him.

Then He said, "If you want to let me know how much you *love* and *appreciate* what I did for you at Calvary, then *rejoice and be glad! Worship and praise and thank Me."* I knelt there for a few more seconds, feeling rather foolish and embarrassed. But I stopped crying immediately. Then I began to worship and praise Him and love Him.

After that night, I have thought many times about what the Lord said to me. You know, Jesus came to this earth for the *sole purpose* of giving His life for us. **For God so loved the world, that he gave his only begotten Son** (John 3:16a). He gave His Son for us. But, Jesus was *willing* to come.

It says in Hebrews 12:2b, **. . . who for the joy that was set before him endured the cross.** He also told those who were following Him, as He was carrying the cross to Golgotha, **Weep not for me, but weep for yourselves, and for your children** (Luke 23:28).

Even though we may shed tears when we read about what Jesus did for us at Calvary or see a movie about His life, we should focus on the fact that the cross is bare, the tomb is empty, and Jesus is alive! He now sits at the right hand of our Father God, who has put all things under His feet. I learned to rejoice and thank Him for His death, burial, and resurrection. Praise be to God.

Once you have the *revelation* of what Jesus did for you on Calvary, you may weep, but you will be crying tears of joy. God wants you to accept what He did for you at Calvary and receive Him as your Lord and Savior, but then you should rejoice and be exceedingly glad that He is alive. Because He lives, you can live also!

Chapter Three

MY CHILD, WHAT DO YOU WANT OF ME?

And Jesus answering saith unto them, Have faith in God. Therefore I say unto you, What things soever ye desire, when ye pray, believe that ye receive them, and ye shall have them.

Mark 11:22,24

Early in our ministry, we had need of everything. Not that we don't have needs now, but I have learned how to pray *specifically* for those needs. Let me share with you how I learned.

One morning as I was praying (and I use that word loosely) I was actually agonizing over the bills and things we needed. I was not agonizing in *intercession* or *faith*, but trying to let God know what bad shape we were in! I was lying prostrate before the Lord in our bedroom with my face in the carpet, crying, "Oh God...oh Lord...I don't know what we are going to do...Oh God, help us...moan...groan...."

The Lord listened to me for awhile. Then all of a sudden He spoke to me. Yes, I heard Him audibly. I have since learned that it was the voice of the Holy Spirit speaking out of my spirit, but it sounded like He was standing right behind me (like God and young Samuel in the Old Testament). He said, "My child, *what* do you want of me?" Well, it so shocked me that I sat upright on my knees and my mind began to race. I had a million thoughts in a flash. He had asked me a question and He wanted an answer. What could I say? What do we need? The only word that came out of my mouth was, "Money." That seemed to sum it all up!

He then left as quickly and quietly as He came. He just wanted to know what I wanted! I was so excited that I got up and ran through the house saying, "He talked to me! God talked to me!" No one was there to hear me, but I had to tell somebody. So I told myself!

Later, the Lord began to reveal to me how to pray correctly, specifically, and effectively. First of all, you go to the Father in the Name of Jesus and make your requests — prayers, supplications, petitions — known. Then you believe that you receive when you pray, and if you have ought against any person, you forgive them. You must know that you are righteous through Jesus and go to Him boldly.

He gave me the example of a lawyer going before a judge with a petition. I had once worked for an attorney, so I could understand His illustration. He said, "The lawyer makes his petition known. He speaks clearly and precisely, and he certainly doesn't moan and groan. The judge then rules according to what he has heard." So it is with the Lord. He answers your prayers when you come to Him in faith, confessing His Word over your situation or problem. You don't go to the Lord like you would your doctor, telling Him all of your problems, aches, and woes. He already knows what you need.

Stand on His Word in the area where you need help. Be specific.

Make a prayer list and stick to it. Don't pray a scatter-load prayer. Pray for what you specifically need and what you are specifically believing for, one thing at a time.

After you have prayed, you will need patience for the answer. You have to learn to wait on the Lord. Psalm 27:14a says to wait on the Lord. The Hebrew word for "wait" means, "be still, relax, be quiet." As long as your prayer lines up with His Word, He will answer at the right time, His time. You might as well relax and **let patience have her perfect work, that ye may be perfect and entire, wanting nothing** (James 1:4)!

Most of all, develop a love relationship with God, your Father. Get to know Him and you will have an unshakable confidence in Him and His Word.

I have been praying specifically for a number of years and can honestly say I have seen overwhelming results. For example, a few years ago I began confessing for an airplane. In the natural, there was no way we could afford a plane and we did not need one at the time, but I felt impressed to confess for one. I also prayed for a pilot. Two years later an airplane was given to us. At the same time, a man and his family joined our church, and he just happened to be a pilot! Incidentally, he is still our pilot today.

Pray specifically and you will get specific answers. Let your petitions be made known to God, for He will fulfill them. Petitions are just requests or prayers. Always remember that He hears you, He loves you, and He *wants* to meet your needs. Then you must stand fast and not waiver. Wait on the Lord and He will bring your confession of His Word to pass.

Chapter Four

DEAR LORD, WOULD YOU FILL MY CUP 'TIL IT OVERFLOWS

I love them that love me; and those that seek me early shall find me.

Proverbs 8:17

When I was about seven years old, my family moved to a house in the country on my grandfather's property, close to Hickory Flat, Mississippi. Even though we only lived there about a year, some of my fondest childhood memories are from that time. It was there that I met Jesus.

That day is still vivid in my memory. It was on a Sunday morning that I sat in the second pew of the Ebenezer Methodist Church, listening to a man named Willie Cook give a testimony of how the Lord had "filled his cup until it overflowed." As he gave the testimony, tears rolled down his cheeks. I was so drawn to him and wanted so much to experience what he had experienced. I didn't know that it was *salvation*.

That night when my sisters and I got on our knees to say our prayers before going to bed, I lingered a little longer. I said to the Lord, "Dear Lord, would You fill my cup 'til it overflows like you did Mr. Cook?" I waited and nothing happened.

I prayed again. "Lord, would you please fill my cup 'til it overflows like you did Mr. Cook?" The Lord knew my heart was sincere, so He answered my prayer and began to pour His beautiful liquid love into my cup (my heart) until I felt like it would burst! I was so thrilled and excited, I began to cry and laugh at the same time.

I jumped in bed and tried to tell my sisters what had just happened to me. I don't think they understood what I was trying to say. I really didn't know how to explain it, except to say that the Lord had filled my cup 'til it overflowed! The Lord came into my heart that night and made me a new creation. I had a new Spirit within me. My feet were now set on a new course, a course that would one day take me to heaven. I was born again!

The following year we moved to Pontotoc, Mississippi, and started attending the First Baptist Church. One Sunday morning when the pastor gave the altar call, my sister Shirley went down to accept Jesus as her Savior. When she stepped out into the aisle, I stepped out right behind her and we walked to the front. We both confessed Jesus as our Lord and were baptized in water.

I often think how the Holy Spirit drew me to Him in a Methodist church. I was saved at home by my bedside. Later I confessed Him publicly and was baptized in water in a Baptist church, and both my parents were raised in the Church of God. In fact, my father's father was a Church of God minister. After I was grown, I went to an Assemblies of God church and was baptized in the Holy Spirit there.

With a background like that, it is easy to see why Agape Church is nondenominational! But you know, the title of a denomination makes no difference. Where the Spirit of the Lord is makes the difference.

For ye are all the children of God by faith in Christ Jesus.
Galatians 3:26

There were times in my life when I did not live for Jesus like I should have, times when I fell down. But He has always been there to encourage me to get back up and keep on walking with Him. He has never forsaken me. He has never stopped loving me. He has always been merciful and kind and faithful. That's why I love Him so. I agree with the Apostle Peter. Jesus is, indeed, precious. (See 1 Pet. 2:7.)

If you haven't already, why don't you ask God to fill your cup 'til it overflows? He will — and you will be gloriously changed!

Chapter Five

YOU TWO ARE JUST OUT ON A LARK

If ye abide in me, and my words abide in you, ye shall ask what ye will, and it shall be done unto you.

John 15:7

By the summer of 1974, Happy and I both had resigned from our jobs to go into the full-time ministry. Our son, Ronnie, was out of school for the summer and we were on the East Coast singing and giving testimony of the great things God had done in our lives.

We were staying with my sister Elizabeth, who lived in Annadale, Virginia. Actually, she booked us in several churches, since we didn't know anybody. We were booked for the summer and everything was just wonderful.

Then one day a dark cloud came over me and the devil said, "You two are just out on a lark. You both resigned good paying jobs. Sure, you have bookings now, but what are you going to do this fall? Nobody knows you; nobody wants you. Ronnie has to start back to school. What are you going to do about him?" Ronnie played drums for us and was a very vital part of the ministry. We called ourselves the "Agape Singers." So I began to worry and fret. What were we going to do? How were we going to pay our bills? What did our future hold?

I went to our little Dodge van to pray and talk to God about these things. The van was our prayer closet on the road. I fell on my knees and asked God every question the devil had asked me! After praying, I felt impressed to read my Bible. Many times God answers me directly through His Word.

I opened the Bible to Matthew, chapter 6. In those days I had no idea what was in chapter 6, but I began reading. The first few verses were dealing with hypocrites. I said, "Oh Lord, I certainly don't feel like I'm a hypocrite!" He said, "Keep on reading."

Finally, I came to the Scriptures to which He was directing me. When I got to verse 25, the words became illuminated and went straight into my heart. God was saying to me through His Word, "Jeanne, don't take thought about what you will do this fall. Don't take thought about Ronnie's schooling. Don't take thought about your house payment, your groceries, your clothes. Don't take thought about anything. Just put Me first in every area of your life and I will take care of you."

That did it! As long as He was first in everything, I didn't have to take thought or worry about anything. What a comfort that was. What a revelation! That was revealed to me many years ago, and it is still working today.

If the Word is not working in your life, check up on yourself. Is He really first in every area of your life? The Word works for *whosoever will* and *you are a whosoever!*

I encourage you to read Matthew 6:25-34 and let it become a revelation in your heart. Don't doubt Him, just trust Him. I have found it gives Him pleasure to not only meet your needs, but to give you the desires of your heart.

Chapter Six

PEACE IN THE TIME OF TROUBLE

These things I have spoken unto you, that in me ye might have *peace*. In the world ye shall have tribulation: but be of good cheer; I have overcome the world.

John 16:33

For many years I have experienced and enjoyed living in the peace of God. Since I have found out that He was *for* me and not *against* me, I have tapped into His peace many times and He has always been there. Today, I understand His peace even more fully and know that only He can give it when all hell breaks loose around me.

On October 16, 1989, I was riding down West Markham Street in Little Rock at 11:15 a.m. with my husband, who was driving. All of a sudden our car just died. We had plenty of gas and the car was in tip-top condition, yet it died. Happy was hurriedly trying to start it as it was coasting to a stop. All I could think to say was, "Get it out of the street!" In fact, that is the last thing I remember saying.

About that time, the driver of a large tire truck behind us plowed into the rear of our car because he wasn't looking where he was going. He literally took a bite out of it, leaving only half of a car. It was totaled and sold for junk.

When he hit us, we hit the dash. Then the thrust of our bodies broke the front seats as we fell back flat. In other words, we were hurled forward then thrown backward. Thank God we weren't thrown through the windshield. At that point, I was knocked unconscious.

The next thing I remember was being put into the ambulance on a stretcher. I felt terrific pain in my back. I couldn't imagine where I was or what had happened; the medical reports say that I had temporary amnesia. But, I had a peace — a peace that was almost awesome. I had absolutely no fear, and I felt God's presence with me.

At the hospital, as I was going in and out of consciousness, I heard Happy telling a policeman what had happened, so I knew for the first time what this was all about. My clothes were full of glass and, as they were stripping them off, two pieces of glass got in my eye, so I had to tell the nurse to get them out.

They took quite a few X-rays, did a CAT scan, and determined the injury to my spine. The medical reports reflect that I sustained three fractured vertebrae (C5, 6 and 7). The most problematic and dangerous fracture of all was T7 (thoracic spine) which had a severe compression fracture of 80%, causing a loss of one inch in my height anteriorly. I had a huge knot on my head and bruises on my body. Happy was banged up a bit, but praise God, his injuries weren't serious.

I could sense they were concerned about whether or not I might be paralyzed. They kept having me move parts of my body and asked constantly if I felt numb anywhere. I remember thinking, "I'm fine." I said over and over, **"No weapon formed against me shall prosper"** (Is. 54:17). The Word of God poured out of my mouth. I told everyone when I was conscious, "I'm a quick healer." I never had anything but the peace of God through it all. It was a calm assurance that all was well.

The doctors wanted to put three rods in my back to support my vertebrae column, but I chose not to have the surgery. Instead, I looked to my Great Physician for total restoration. The doctors told me if I didn't have the surgery, I would be in the hospital flat on my back for two weeks and at home in bed for at least three months. I would not be able to get out of bed for anything and would have to wear a back brace.

Of course, I did not receive that report. I knew in my heart that God would supernaturally take care of me. Many great men and women of God prayed for me, adding their faith to ours. Therefore, I knew that *I was healed by the stripes of Jesus!*

Someone sent me a card with a poem on it that says it the way I see it:

> *The One who made us*
> *knows how to mend us.*
> *He is the Great Physician —*
> *the only One who can heal*
> *body, soul, and spirit.*
> *His appointment calendar*
> *is never too full...*
> *His schedule is never too busy...*
> *His diagnosis is accurate...*
> *His treatment is gentle...*

His results are wonderful!
You couldn't be
in better hands!

I'm so thankful for all the believers who ministered such love to me. Many called, sent cards, food, flowers, gifts, or prayed for me. Daily I was refreshed and blessed and overwhelmed by the love and compassion of God's children.

The first couple of days in the hospital, my back was in a lot of pain. But all I could think of was the excruciating pain my Jesus suffered for me on Calvary. My pain was so minute compared to His, and He opened not His mouth. I began to praise and thank Him, identifying in a very small measure with His pain. What a wonderful Savior we have. He is Lord over every situation. I left the hospital after a little over a week, and shortly after that my total healing was manifested.

Some of you may be saying to yourselves, "How did this happen to you?" Or, "Did you open the door somewhere to the devil?" Well, don't think I haven't searched my heart and sought God about this! After prayer, I can honestly say that my heart was right before God.

I have since realized that the Holy Spirit did try to keep us from leaving our house that day, but we did not perceive it was Him. I thought because I didn't want to rush to get dressed and meet my uncle for lunch that what I was "feeling" was just me. That is where we faith people miss it. We can make our faith confessions for protection, but if the Holy Spirit tells you not to do something, you had better obey Him!

I do believe this accident was an attack of the enemy not just to steal the love and trust I have toward my Father God, but also to steal the Word I had sown in my heart and the hearts of other believers. One of my favorite subjects to teach is the love of God and how He protects and leads us by His Spirit.

Don't let the devil steal the Word that is in your heart! Mark 4:14-20 says that the sower soweth the *Word*, and *Satan comes* immediately to steal the *Word* that was sown. It says that affliction and persecution arise for the *Word's* sake. He would like to make you believe that you can't depend on God. If he succeeds, he can control and manipulate you. He wants to *choke the Word* out of you and me.

But he can't! I am good ground. I am still alive! I am still in control, and without God's protection I would be dead. The devil can't steal the Word out of my heart. Don't let him steal it out of yours.

You too can know that same *peace* of God that passes all understanding (Phil. 4:7) even when you are in a great trial of affliction. You can have peace when you truly see God as your Father, and when you love Him and His Word more than anyone or anything else in the world. The Bible has many Scriptures which talk about the peace of God that is available to you. If the revelation of this truth becomes a reality in your life, you will live in His peace — no matter what challenges and trials you face.

Chapter Seven

I LOVE YOU, GOD...

Know therefore that the Lord thy God, he is God, the faithful God, which keepeth covenant and mercy with them that love him and keep his commandments to a thousand generations.

Deuteronomy 7:9

One day as I was sharing with a friend how I stood on God's Word for healing, I said, "I just trust the Lord because I love Him. When you truly love God, you will have faith in His Word." I thought nothing more about the statement until the next morning. I was listening to a tape on the subject of healing, where the following Scripture was quoted, **Faith worketh by love** (Gal. 5:6). My spirit leaped inside of me when I realized that my faith works because I love God! How simple, how miraculous.

However, I have not always loved God. Let me tell you why. My father was accidentally killed when I was a young girl, and my pastor told me that God had taken my daddy because He needed him in heaven. I thought to myself, "What about my mother? What about my sisters and me? Surely we need our daddy more."

At that point, resentment, bitterness, and anger toward God entered my heart. I felt as if God were someone in whom I could neither rely nor trust. After all, my daddy was a godly man. He was a Sunday School superintendent. He always took us to church. He was everything a wife or child could ask for. We had a happy home and I loved him dearly.

When he died happiness drained out of our lives like water out of a tub. Instead of laughter, sorrow filled our hearts. How could you love a God Who could cause this kind of heartache?

It is strange, but I continued going to church, sang in the choir, and did everything a Christian is supposed to do. But I did not *love* God. I served Him out of fear. I never knew when He might decide to take me, and I feared going to hell. I had a friend who would say to me, "Oh Jeanne, God is love." I would say, "No, He is a God of wrath." I honestly felt that way about Him.

I loved *Jesus* because He was sweet and kind and went about doing good. However, I never felt this way about God. I heard a preacher say one time that churches are filled with people who do not love God. They fear Him or follow religious traditions that include Him, but what they secretly think is that He has taken their child, husband or wife, mother or father, or something they treasure. They resent Him just as I did. It is a sad truth.

It wasn't until Happy got saved in 1972, when we started attending a home Bible study, that I learned the truth about God. We were studying E. W. Kenyon's Basic Bible Course called *The Bible in Light of Our Redemption*. One evening the statement was made that Satan was the god of this world who came to rob, steal, and kill, and that God was not the author of these things.

I thought out loud, "You mean God didn't take my daddy?" The

Bible study leaders asked me when and how he died. I told them he was electrocuted when he was 36 years old while putting up a television antenna. They said, "Oh no, God did not do that. It is God's will that we live long on this earth, and not only that, He wants us to be prosperous and healthy."

They continued to tell me how Satan had become the god of this world through the fall of Adam, and that he goes about through the earth seeking whom he may devour. Man has a choice to serve God or reject Him, but God will always love man. God is a good God. There is no darkness in Him whatsoever. He is light.

After hearing this good news, it *felt* right. That sounded like what God ought to be like! I had an all-consuming desire to know God. I figured I could learn about Him in the Old Testament, so I began to read it. I totally fell in love with God while reading the Old Testament! I saw Him as a God Who loved His people so much and did everything He could to protect and guide them. I saw Him as He really was, not as I had been taught.

After reading and meditating, I put down my Bible, looked up toward heaven, and with tears streaming down my face said, "Oh God, please forgive me for all the bad things I've said about You through the years. Forgive me for not knowing You. Forgive me for not loving You. I'm so sorry, God. I want You to know I love You." As soon as I finished speaking, He spoke back to me with such love and compassion. He said, "*I love you, Jeanne.*"

His love flowed through me like rivers of living water. Three times I told Him I loved Him, and three times He answered that He loved me too. I have not been the same since! No man, no devil, nothing can steal the love that I have for my Father God.

Friend, if you have ought in your heart today toward God for something you *think* He did to you, release it now and ask Him to forgive you. Get that bitterness and resentment out of your heart. It will only hurt you. You just don't know the peace and joy you can live in when your heart is right with God, your Father. My prayer is that you let His love flow through you today.

Chapter Eight

GOD, WHY DID YOU LET THAT HAPPEN?

But God, who is rich in mercy, for his great love wherewith he loved us, even when we were dead in sins, hath quickened us [made us alive] together with Christ, (by grace are ye saved;) And hath raised us up together, and made us sit together in heavenly places in Christ Jesus.

Ephesians 2:4-6

Being the wife of a pastor, I have had the opportunity and pleasure to minister to many people through counseling, prayer, and deliverance. It has given me great joy to see people set free by the Word and power of God. I have learned, however, not to be shocked or carry the burden of some of the things I hear, because so many people are suffering from the bondages of sin and Satan.

I remember when we first started Agape Church in 1979, a beautiful woman was saved and started attending our church with her seven-year-old son. She was married, but her husband was not saved and did not come to church with her. She came to see me one day and poured her heart out about things in which she had been involved. She wanted deliverance from those *strongholds* in her life.

As I was praying for her, all of a sudden she said, "Incest." I said, "Are you a victim of incest? Did your father abuse you?" "No," she said, "I have sex with my son." When she said that, I reeled with shock. I had to control myself to keep from showing my feelings. After all, she had come to me for help.

In the seventies, incest was not talked about as openly as it is today. Also, I had never dealt with a mother-son sexual relationship and I was shocked and grieved — perhaps all the more so because I had a son.

I finished praying for her the best I could, and she went home rejoicing in the Lord and gloriously set free. However, I went home with the burden of what I had just heard! All I could do was think about that poor little innocent boy and weep. I tried to put these thoughts out of my mind, but they just kept coming back. I tried to read the Word, but my eyes were blinded by tears.

Finally I got angry at God for letting something like this happen. I said, *"God, why did You let that happen to that little boy. I can't stand it. How can You stand it?"*

Around midnight the Lord got me out of bed and said He wanted me to write down what He was about to tell me. He took me to Genesis 6:5-7, which says, **And God saw that the wickedness of man was great in the earth, and that every imagination of the thoughts of his heart was only evil continually. And it repented the Lord that he had made man on the earth, and it grieved him at his heart.**

God said to me, "My heart is bigger than your heart. My grief is greater than your grief." I immediately felt ashamed for accusing

Him of not caring. At once, I asked for His forgiveness.

God continued to minister to me. Adam was created in God's image; his blood was charged with the life of God. When he sinned, his blood became cursed, and this curse was passed to all mankind. Man, since Adam's fall, was evil, unholy, and without natural affection.

God was so grieved He said He was going to destroy man, whom He had created. In the great flood, He did except for Noah and his family, who had found grace in His sight. But that did not stop the evil in man's heart and mind. God became so *grieved* over the sin of incest that He made over 20 laws against it in Leviticus, Deuteronomy, and other books of the Bible. There were stiff penalties for this kind of perversion.

None of you shall approach to any that is near of kin to him, to uncover their nakedness: I am the Lord.

Leviticus 18:6

("Uncover their nakedness" in this verse means sexual intercourse.) The only hope for man was a redeemer, but before Jesus came God instituted the blood covenant. Once a year, the blood of bulls and goats was sacrificed by the high priest to cover the sins of the people. This prepared the way for Jesus, Who was willing to come and once and for all take the sins of the world upon Himself.

Jesus shed His blood for the remission of all sin. Because His blood was pure and holy and not corrupt, He was the *only* One Who could redeem man. Jesus shed His blood for us and presented it to the Father. *Now God sees us through Jesus' sinless Blood.*

Jesus stands as a mediator between lost man and God. (1 Tim. 2:5) For those of us who are saved, He stands as an intercessor.

(Rom. 8:34) When we accept Jesus as Lord and Savior, we receive a *new* nature, a nature that does not desire to sin. The Lord told me, "Now I see man through the eyes of Jesus and My heart is not grieved. Otherwise, I could not stand the sin either."

God, by giving His Son, has done all He is going to do about sins here on earth, including all sexual sins. He has given to us, as His children, the responsibility to teach people how to live according to the Word, to reveal the devices of Satan and his demonic warfare, and to resist the devil. Most of all, He has given us the responsibility to teach people that God loves them and is interceding for them. He told me, "Don't carry the burden. Jesus already did. Pray for the abused children, and let God love them through you."

Chapter Nine

LORD, ARE WE ON THE RIGHT TRACK?

My son, attend to my words; incline thine ear unto my sayings. Let them not depart from thine eyes; keep them in the midst of thine heart. For they are life unto those that find them, and health to all their flesh. Keep thy heart with all diligence; for out of it are the issues of life. Put away from thee a froward [crooked] mouth, and perverse lips put far from thee.

Proverbs 4:20-24

I had been a Christian for many years when Happy got saved on February 11, 1972. However, my walk as a Christian was anything but joyous! It seemed like when everything was going well, a catastrophe would be just around the corner. And I didn't always know how to deal with these catastrophes according to the Word. In fact, I had never been taught how to *overcome* in this life. I thought, "Well, Satan did that," or "This is God's will," but I never knew there was anything I could do about it.

After Happy got saved, we started attending a home Bible study every Friday night. In this meeting, there were wonderful charismatics, full of the love of God. We started studying E. W. Kenyon's *Basic Bible Study*. While Happy was learning God's Word, I was relearning. Although I had been taught a lot of good things, I had many *traditions and doctrines of men* that I had to deal with. It was a real awakening, to say the least.

There were other books that were introduced to me: Kenneth E. Hagin's books *Authority of the Believer* (I never knew I *had* authority), *Right and Wrong Thinking,* and his writings about demons which forever changed my life.

Of course, Charles Capps' books on the confession of the tongue and Kenneth Copeland's books on faith and prosperity just had me walking on cloud nine. For the first time in my Christian life, I was walking in a joy and freedom I had never known. I said one day, "God, you are just too good to be true!"

During this time, however, the Word of faith and the prosperity message was not being received in denominational churches. I began to hear many negative things about what I was learning. People were telling me that this teaching was off balance and not the truth. They even said that it was of the devil. You name it, they said it.

Eventually, I became really disturbed about all I was hearing, for most of it was coming from good Christian people. So I got on my knees beside the bed and earnestly prayed, "Lord, are we on the right track? We don't want to get off on any kind of false doctrine, so please God, direct us in the way we should go. Please don't let us get off balance."

All of a sudden the Holy Spirit rose up in me and began asking *me* questions. He said, "Jeanne, have you ever *loved Me* like you do now?" I said, "No, Lord. You know I had to learn to love You because I didn't *know* You." He said, "Have you ever been as *healthy* as you are right now?" I said, "No, Lord. You know I always had colds or the flu every year. I've never known such health." He said, "Have you ever known such *peace?*" I said, "Oh no, Lord. Never have I walked in such peace."

He continued, "Have you ever known such *joy?*" I said, "Oh my no, Lord. I've never been so happy in my walk with You." He said, "Have you ever read My *Word* like you do now?" I said, "No, Lord. You know it used to be a real effort to read Your Word, but now I devour it!" He said, "Have you every been as *prosperous?*" I said, "No, Lord. I can honestly say You have blessed me like I've never been blessed before." Then He said so profoundly, "Well, wouldn't you say you were on the right track then?"

I jumped up and said, "Yes! Praise God, and never again will I ever doubt that *You* are all the *Word* says You are, and that You will keep me on the right track. I long for truth above all things. I will not be double-minded about Your Word or tossed to and fro with every wind of doctrine. I will be established in Your Word."

That was many years ago, and I'm still walking in the joy of the Lord. All His blessings are mine — and they are yours as well! He has never failed me, and He will never fail you either.

Set a goal to be a success according to God's Word, knowing that He wants you to be a success. He is your source. Seek Him instead of things. Obey Him. Don't take anxious thoughts or say wrong things. Don't grieve your spirit by speaking words that are contrary to the Word of God that is hidden in your heart.

It may take awhile to change the image you have of yourself. But seeing yourself the way God sees you will build you up and give you strength.

Don't be afraid to step out and believe God for all He has made available to you. You will be surprised at how your life will change. You can have a little preview of what heaven is all about — a little heaven on earth.

Yes, God is too good to be true...but He is!

Chapter Ten

USE YOUR OWN FAITH

Cast not away therefore your confidence, which hath great re-compense of reward. For ye have need of patience, that, after ye have done the will of God, ye might receive the promise.

Hebrews 10:35-36

In the early days of our ministry, the motto in our household was, "Every man for himself." If any of us needed or wanted anything, we had to believe God for it. It was a walk of faith, for sure!

You may remember my article in chapter 1, "But Father, I'm A Second-Hand Anna." The story described in this chapter happened about two months later.

I was continuing to believe God for clothes, as well as other things we needed for the ministry. I was quoting the Word and thanking God daily for His blessings and for the manifestation of my prayers.

One day a lady came up to me in church and said, "My sister owns a dress shop in another town and she wants to give you a new dress. If you will take the time to go see her, I know she will bless you." About two weeks later, I drove down to see her. I was very excited about the new dress!

When I arrived at the dress shop, the lady was very kind. She started bringing things for me to try on. I picked out a dress and told her which one I wanted. She said, "Oh, I want to give you more than just one." I was so flabbergasted and thrilled I could hardly speak. At any rate, after all was said and done, I came home with three dresses and two pantsuits — all beautiful and brand new.

I was beside myself. I could hardly wait for Happy and Ronnie to see how God had blessed me. I laid the clothes out ever so neatly on the bed, so that when they came in they couldn't help but see everything. I wanted to see their reaction.

But their reaction was different than what I had expected. They both peered into the bedroom from the hallway as if they couldn't walk on in and said pitifully, "Where's ours?" I said, "Use your own faith!"

That may seem harsh to you, but like I said before, in our household it was *every man for himself.* We each had to believe God, using and developing our *individual* faith. After all, each person *is* accountable for what they do with their *own* faith.

The Bible says, **Without faith it is impossible to please God** (Heb. 11:6). I don't know about you, but I want to please Him! One of the ways we can please Him is to trust Him and act on our faith.

There are many examples in the Bible of men and women with different levels of faith. Jesus told some they had *great faith* and others they had *weak* or *little faith*. He told the centurion, **I have not**

found so *great faith*, no, not in Israel (Matt. 8:10b). Jesus was amazed when this Gentile man simply asked Him with such great faith to speak the Word only. Jesus said, **As thou hast believed, so be it done unto thee** (Matt. 8:13).

Another time, a woman of Canaan came to Jesus asking Him to heal her daughter who was vexed with a devil. He said, **It is not meet to take the children's** (Jews) **bread, and to cast it to dogs** (Gentiles) (Matt. 15:26). But she worshiped Him and said, **Truth, Lord: yet the dogs eat of the crumbs which fall from their master's table** (Matt. 15:27). Jesus answered, **O woman, great is thy faith: be it unto thee even as thou wilt** (Matt. 15:28). Notice that each time He found faith, He was moved to action.

There are other occasions of great feats of faith in the Bible. There was the leper, the blind man, and the woman with the issue of blood. However, Jesus did not comment on their *great faith*. But He did comment on those occasions where He saw *little faith*.

In Matthew, Jesus said to not take thought or worry about anything, that He would take care of you, **O ye of little faith.** (Matt. 6:25-34.) Then one day the disciples went into a ship, and when they came to the middle of the sea, a great storm came up and covered the ship with water. Jesus was asleep in the boat. His disciples awakened Him, thinking they were going to die. He said, **Why are ye fearful, O ye of little faith** (Matt. 8:26)?

Another time, when Peter was walking on the water to meet Jesus, he saw the boisterous wind and began to sink, crying, "Lord, save me." Jesus saved him but said, **O thou of little faith, wherefore didst thou doubt?** (Matt. 14:31). One time when Jesus was warning His disciples against false doctrine, He also said, **O ye of little faith...** (Matt. 16:8).

We can clearly see from these passages that God wants us to trust Him totally, without reservation and without fear, in every area of our lives. We can't even be born again until we trust and receive Him through faith. Everything in this life requires faith. In fact, the subject of faith alone could fill up the pages of many books. It is important to know that the Lord *expects each one of us to exercise our faith* and grow in our faith walk with Him.

The Lord spoke to me one night during a Believer's Convention in Fort Worth, Texas, while Brother Kenneth Copeland was preaching. The Lord told me that if I had not used my faith for clothes and other things I needed early in the ministry, I never would have been able to believe Him for the church that we built and paid for, not to mention the many other areas of ministry where we had to believe God or sink. He told me to never stop my faith projects, because they keep my faith alive and working.

If you will learn to trust God for the small things in life, you can and will believe Him in greater areas. You will believe God for the supernatural. You will believe God for things thought impossible. You can, by developing your faith, have great confidence in Him and His Word. You will do great exploits for Him on this earth!

In time my little family did use their own faith, and they were blessed just as I was. So my friend, I say to you, *"Use your own faith!"*

Chapter Eleven

OUR RIGHTEOUSNESS IS AS FILTHY RAGS

And be found in him, not having mine own righteousness, which is of the law, but that which is through the faith of Christ, the righteousness which is of God by faith.

Philippians 3:9

In 1973 during a Bible study, I heard a lady say, "We are the righteousness of God." When she said it, I responded by saying, "Our righteousness is as filthy rags." She looked at me and said, "Yes Jeanne, *our* righteousness is as filthy rags, but I'm not talking about our righteousness. I'm talking about *His* righteousness, in us through Jesus Christ."

I perceived immediately that I needed to shut my mouth because I was showing my spiritual ignorance! The pitiful thing is, I really did not know that I was righteous in Christ Jesus. I thought I was an unworthy worm in the dust. In fact, I used to sing a song entitled, "Unworthy," and could I ever get into that song! You see, in my mind I *was* unworthy, because in church I had been taught all my life that I was.

I don't believe I ever heard a message taught that told me I had been made the righteousness of God. Therefore, I was sin-conscious, not righteousness-minded. When you are sin-conscious, you sin. You also think sickness instead of health, weakness instead of strength, failure instead of success, poverty instead of prosperity, and defeat instead of victory.

Unfortunately, the Church has developed some wrong religious ideas about righteousness. Just what is righteousness and how do we get it? Do we work for it? Sacrifice for it? Fast for it? Beg for it? *No!*

Thank God, through Jesus and faith in Him we *become* righteous. (See Rom. 5:17-19.) It is a gift that cannot be earned. Righteousness is the ability to stand in the Father's presence without the sense of guilt, condemnation, or inferiority.

When I found out that I was the righteousness of God through faith in Jesus, it utterly destroyed my sin-consciousness. I understood that it was His righteousness, not mine. I realized that I had been *made* righteous through Him. That was one revelation, if not *the* revelation, that changed my life and set me free. He was in me. In me were His abilities, His strength, and His authority.

I Corinthians 15:34a says, **Awake to righteousness, and sin not.** Well, I did wake up and I have been walking in His righteousness ever since! I know that I am in right standing with God and justified (just as if I had never sinned). It's not that I deserved this gift — it was His grace, His love, and His unmerited favor.

When you know who you are in God, it changes you. All of a sudden you feel accepted by Him, even with all your faults. You realize just how much He loves you and that He is for you, not against you.

Now I can come to Him with full assurance of that love and right standing. I walk with Him in that authority every day. I am a new creation, a conqueror, an overcomer, a joint-heir with Jesus.

So friend, awake to righteousness! Get a revelation of what Jesus' sacrifice did for you at Calvary. Put on your breastplate of righteousness and wear it victoriously!

Chapter Twelve
WHAT'S YOUR SIGN?

Neither shall ye use enchantment, nor observe times....
Regard not them that have familiar spirits, neither seek after wizards, to be defiled by them: I am the Lord your God.

Leviticus 19:26b,31

In the sixties, horoscopes (prophesying a person's future through the use of astrology) were on the rise. Everyone wanted to know what astrological sign you were born under. It was the topic of conversation during coffee breaks and at lunch tables. Everywhere you went, people were talking about their "signs."

I was no different. I worked in an office where we all discussed each other's signs. Some read books about astrology or followed their daily horoscopes in the newspaper. Many had faith in them. I personally did not believe that anyone or anything could chart my course in life but God. Even so, horoscopes were fun to play with and an interesting conversation piece. How foolish, deceived, and spiritually ignorant I was!

I was deceived to the fact that prophesying the future through horoscopes was of the devil. I rationalized that if everyone was born around the same time of the month, it stood to reason they might have certain personality traits in common. And after all, the wise men followed a *star* to find Jesus.

No one ever showed me Scriptures that said this practice was of the devil. I even told my pastor what his sign was and read his horoscope to him. He just smiled really big and had me look up his wife's! He was a godly man, but he did not know what the Bible said about it either.

After Happy got saved and we started attending a Bible study, my eyes were opened. Some of the couples would get together for dinner before the meeting. One night as we were eating, I said to one of the ladies, "Beverly, what sign are you?" Her mouth dropped open, her eyes popped out, and she said, "Jeanne, that stuff is of the devil."

I immediately looked away, embarrassed and angry. I didn't say anything (praise the Lord). I thought to myself, "See if I talk to you anymore." And of course, I did. She was a precious lady whom I still love and respect.

Shortly afterward, Happy and I went to a service where Hilton Sutton was teaching on the subject of familiar spirits. He went into great detail, reading Scriptures on witchcraft, astrology, and sorcery, pointing out God's warnings against them. He read from Deuteronomy:

> **There shall not be found among you any one that...useth divination, or an observer of times, or an enchanter, or a witch. Or a charmer, or a consulter with familiar spirits, or a wizard, or a necromancer.**

> **For all that do these things are an abomination unto the Lord...For these nations, which thou shalt possess, hearkened unto observers of times, and unto diviners: but as for thee, the Lord thy God hath not suffered thee so to do. The Lord thy God will raise up unto thee a Prophet from the midst of thee, of thy brethren, like unto me; unto him ye shall hearken.**
> **Deuteronomy 18:10-12a,14-15**

When I saw in the Word that horoscopes were an abomination to God, I was shocked and convicted to my toes. Brother Sutton asked those who needed deliverance from any of these things to come to the front for prayer. Needless to say, I made haste to get down there. I renounced any participation or involvement with the occult, because astrology is a part of it. I was delivered from it all. From that day forward, I have avoided anything having to do with astrology.

The New Age movement that has swept America is steeped in occult-based practices. It is a mixture of Eastern mysticism and Western occultism. Its deep involvement in practices like divination, witchcraft, sorcery, consulting mediums, spiritism, and numerous other ungodly customs causes demonic forces to be unleashed in our classrooms, on television, on lecture circuits, in print, art, music, business management, children's toys, games, and movies. It is nothing less than a major branch of the prophesied latter-day rise of the antichrist forces.

If you are playing around with horoscopes or any of the things I have mentioned, you are playing with fire and you will get burned. You are opening the door for the enemy to come into your life and you are dishonoring God. Renounce it now, repent of your involvement in the occult, and God will forgive you. He forgave me!

Pray this prayer of deliverance now:

"Father, in the Name of Jesus and according to Your Word, I believe in my heart and say with my mouth that Jesus is the Lord of my life. I repent from and renounce any involvement I have had with the occult, horoscopes, or New Age movement. I confess that from this day forth I am set free and delivered from all dealings with anything that is an abomination to You, in Jesus' Name! Thank You, Lord, for delivering me right now. Amen."

Chapter Thirteen

HOLY SPIRIT, I WANT TO KNOW YOU

Howbeit when He, the Spirit of truth, is come, he will guide you into all truth: for he shall not speak of himself; but whatsoever he shall hear, *that* shall he speak: and he will shew you things to come.
John 16:13

❧

I have shared with you how I came to know and love God. I had a relationship with Jesus, but I did not know or love God, my Father. Once I really came to know Him, I found that He was kind, merciful, compassionate, and a loving Father Who wanted more than anything for His creation to love and worship Him. Having a relationship with God totally changed my life.

One day while meditating on the Word, I realized that I did not know the Person of the Holy Spirit. I knew God the Father and God the Son, but I did not know God the Holy Spirit. I did not know the *power* of the Trinity. I had a longing to know Him too.

So, with this hunger to know the Holy Spirit, His personality and His ways, I said, "Holy Spirit, I want to know You. Please reveal

Yourself to me. I want to recognize Your presence. I want to know Your voice. I want to know You so that You can lead, *guide*, and direct me just as You said You would."

I believe one of the greatest needs of the Church is to understand and have an individual knowledge of the Person of the Holy Spirit. He is not shapeless, a dove, or a cloud. He is not oil, fire, or tongues either. These are only symbols or manifestations of His personality, just as Jesus was sometimes called a "lamb." The important thing is that He is God the Holy Spirit and we can *know* Him. Paul said that he didn't know Jesus after the flesh, but by the Spirit, so we can know Him too.

Shortly after I asked the Holy Spirit to reveal Himself to me, Happy and I were attending a great convention. One day as someone was preaching, the Holy Spirit came upon me and covered me like a blanket with His sweet presence. I began to weep. I couldn't help it. Tears just rolled and rolled down my cheeks. When the Holy Spirit comes upon you, it is a real and tangible presence. You can feel Him. It is the feeling of overwhelming love and compassion. It is joy unspeakable and full of glory.

Then the speaker's words faded to the background as the Holy Spirit began to talk to me. There was no doubt that it was Him. He said, "I want you to know that the faith projects you have had in the past were from Me. I put those things in your heart so you could use your faith and begin to trust God to meet *all* your needs as well as your desires. By using your faith for simple things like clothes, things for your house, things to bless other people, and things for the ministry, you developed an unshakable confidence in God. If you had not believed God for those things, you could never have believed God to build Agape Church and pay for it as it was being built. You could never have believed Him *for the things that really count.* You tried Him and found Him faithful."

You will never know how much that blessed me! Not only did the Holy Spirit reveal His presence to me, but He spoke just the words I needed at that time. You see, for the previous few months I had been hearing people and preachers say that we should not ask God for personal things or personal prosperity. I even heard one very well-known man of God say that he believed the devil answered those kinds of prayers to get people off track and get their minds on things instead of God. As a result, I had backed off my faith projects.

While I do agree that we can get off balance on this kind of praying, I also know that God said He would give us the desires of our hearts, as long as they were in agreement with His Word. I had actually been questioning God on this very thing, so you can see why I was so blessed by what the Holy Spirit said to me.

He came upon me and talked to me at different times the whole week we were in that meeting. He let me sense His presence, then He would speak to me. Therefore, I learned what *His* presence felt like, because there is a counterfeit. I know His voice, and I can distinguish it from the many voices there are in the world. I learned how to listen to Him so I can be led by my spirit.

I don't have room to tell you all the wonderful things I have learned since that time. There are so many mighty manifestations of His divine works. To name a few:

> He was there when the world was spoken into existence.
> He anointed men to write the Bible.
> He plays a vital part in man's salvation.
> He is a comforter, teacher, guide, and counselor.

He gives us strength and makes us bold.
He has a mind, will, and emotions.
He can be grieved and resisted.
He is an encourager and intercessor.
He is the *power* of the Highest.

You can see He is more than just a blessing. He is not just an experience you have had or a feeling to enjoy. He is *real*. He is a *person*. He is the *Spirit of God*.

Once you know Him, you will recognize His presence wherever you go. I remember the first time I went to Austria with Happy for a conference on the Holy Spirit. I could not speak or understand German, but I understood and recognized the tangible, unmistakable presence of the Holy Spirit. It made me feel right at home because I knew Someone who was there! It was beautiful. In fact, when I got up to sing through an interpreter, I told them that very thing.

If you don't know the Person of the Holy Spirit, ask Him to reveal Himself to *you*. He will! But remember that He is very gentle and sensitive. Don't play games with Him. If you truly want to know Him, He will reveal Himself to you marvelously and wondrously. That is His purpose on this earth, to minister life and truth to you and me.

Chapter Fourteen

KEEP YOUR EYES ON ME AND YOU'LL MAKE IT

Let thine eyes look right on, and let thine eyelids look straight before thee. Ponder the path of thy feet, and let all thy ways be established. Turn not to the right hand nor to the left: remove thy foot from evil.

Proverbs 4:25-27

Recently, we had Marilyn Hickey at our church for a "Revelation Encounter" conference. It was a tremendous meeting and really impacted us with biblical knowledge of coming events. As she taught, she showed various filmed scenes to illustrate her points.

One of the pictures showed Satan being thrown into the lake of fire, where the false prophet and the antichrist were. You could see them thrashing about — still alive after a thousand years. That picture brought back vivid memories of a dream I had back in the sixties. I would like to share it with you.

At the time I had the dream, I was not living an overcoming

Christian life. I did not have a revelation that I could overcome in this life. My knowledge of the Word came from what I heard preached, not from a personal study of the Bible. I was taught that I was a sinner saved by grace and that I still had a sin nature; therefore, I could not help but sin.

Later I learned differently. I learned that I have the nature of God inside me and it was just the flesh that I had to deal with. Romans 6:12 says, **Let not sin therefore reign in your mortal body, that ye should obey it in the lusts thereof.** We don't have to sin, but if we do, 1 John 1:9 says, **If we confess our sins, he is faithful and just to forgive us our sins, and to cleanse us from all unrighteousness.**

Back to the dream. One night, without any provocation, I had a dream. It was so vivid and so real that I remember every detail even to this very day. I have since learned that it was a spiritual dream or a night vision.

In the dream I could see myself standing on the side of the earth and it was in flames. People were running to and fro, screaming and pulling their hair, burning alive. I was standing there on planet earth, looking across a great gulf, and I could see heaven on the other side. It looked to be about two blocks away. I saw Jesus standing on the side of heaven with His hands outstretched toward me. He said, "Come." He had on a long white robe and looked so kind and compassionate, so compelling.

While looking at Him, wringing my hands, I said, "I want to come but I can't! I will fall if I try to walk. I'll fall!" (There was no way to get to Him but by walking on thin air.) He said, "Put your eyes on Me. Look straight into My eyes and begin to walk. Don't look to the left or to the right. Don't look back and don't look down. Just keep your eyes on Me and you will make it."

Well, I knew that I didn't want to stay there and burn, so I fastened my eyes on His eyes and took a step, then another, and another. I took one step at a time, one foot in front of the other, with my eyes glued to His. If I had looked away, I would have fallen into outer darkness.

Finally, I made it to the other side — to Jesus! I threw my arms around Him and wept with such joy. He smiled and welcomed me to heaven. Everything was so peaceful, so beautiful, so magnificent. I saw people smiling and talking to one another and, in the distance, I saw a beautiful golden city. It was so wonderful to be there.

Then I awoke. I felt such an overwhelming joy. I felt as if Jesus was telling me that I was going to make it to heaven and He was telling me how. It was later that I learned Jesus is the Word. John 1:14 says, **And the Word was made flesh, and dwelt among us, (and we beheld his glory, the glory as of the only begotten of the Father,) full of grace and truth.** If I kept my eyes fastened on the Word and never let it out of my sight, I would never fall.

I also found out that Proverbs 4:25-27 says almost exactly what He said to me in the dream. At that time, I had no idea that it was even in the Bible. It says, **Let thine eyes look right on, and let thine eyelids look straight before thee. Ponder the path of thy feet, and let all thy ways be established. Turn not to the right hand nor to the left: remove thy foot from evil.**

The Lord does not want us to look back at our failures and sins. He wants us to look straight ahead. He also does not want us to look down, but to hold our heads high because He lives in us. We do not have to be defeated in this life. Through Jesus, we can walk in victory.

If you have felt like a failure and have not been an overcomer in this life, I have good news for you: You can be an overcomer! If you will just keep your eyes on Jesus and His Word, and let Him direct your footsteps each day, not looking to the left or right, not looking back at your mistakes, *you will make it.*

In the early seventies, when Happy and I were traveling and singing in the ministry, we went to a church in Lafayette, Louisiana. I went to their bookstore to look around and saw a painting on the wall that almost blew me away. It was an oil painting of my dream almost to a "T." I ran to Happy crying, "It's my dream! It's my dream! Someone has painted my dream! I want to buy it, no matter what it costs." It was for sale so we bought it.

A few years later, I saw another picture. It also looked a lot like my dream, but it was a little different. It was called "The Way." In it, the earth was in flames and heaven was on the other side with a mighty gulf between them. The difference between this picture and the other was a cross that laid a path between earth and heaven. People were walking across the gulf on the cross. They were in their white robes, going to meet Jesus, Who was standing with His arms outstretched, ready to receive them. When I saw this picture, I realized that in my dream I had a foundation under me and did not know it. It was the cross of Jesus. Praise His matchless Name!

Chapter Fifteen

WHAT ABOUT ME, LORD?

But the fruit of the Spirit is love, joy, peace, longsuffering, gentleness, goodness, faith, meekness, temperance [self-control]; **against such there is no law.**

Galatians 5:22-23

One of the wonderful benefits of knowing God and meditating on His Word is finding out that you can have a happy marriage. People go to marriage counselors and that is fine. They go to marriage seminars and that is wonderful. Some even write Ann Landers. But you can find out what you need to know by reading the Word of God and developing a love for Him. The closer you get to God, the better wife or husband you will be.

Spending time in fellowship and praise daily will perfect those things that pertain to life and godliness in your life *and* marriage. God will show you how to be a delightful partner to your spouse. He cares about these things. After all, He is the One who started the whole business of marriage.

In Genesis 2:18, we read that God said, **It is not good that man should be alone; I will make him an help meet for him.** God first made the animals and Adam named them, but they did not fulfill the loneliness he felt. Believe it or not, a dog is not man's best friend! So, God made a woman for man. Man was not complete until she was made. She is to be his help meet. "Help" means to aid or give assistance to, suitable, qualified, and adaptable. "Meet" means to surround and protect. Therefore, a woman can adapt to any situation, for her makeup is to be understanding. But these qualities in her have to be nurtured. We have to be trained to be a godly help meet. Titus 2:4 says that we have to actually be trained to love our husbands.

You may be thinking, "I do love my husband." Yes, I am sure you do. But most of the time it is a sensual, soulical love, governed by the five physical senses. Agape love, which is unconditional, comes from the recreated spirit, built up and led by the Holy Spirit. The God-kind of love is found in 1 Corinthians 13:4-7:

Charity [agape] suffereth long, and is kind; charity [agape] envieth not; charity [agape] vaunteth not itself, is not puffed up, Doth not behave itself unseemly, seeketh not her own, is not easily provoked, thinketh no evil; Rejoiceth not in iniquity, but rejoiceth in the truth; Beareth all things, believeth all things, hopeth all things, endureth all things.

I learned these things when I began to study the Word for myself. I did not know the first thing about being a godly help meet according to the Word. In fact, I had never heard the words "help meet" before! Unfortunately, there was no preaching on these kinds of things when I was growing up. Thank God things have changed in the last 20 years.

I remember the very first time I was given a book on being a godly wife. I started reading it and became disgusted. When it talked about submitting to our husbands, I thought, "Well, what about me. It looks like I'm supposed to do all the doing and the giving." So I just pitched the book aside and said, "Forget you." But I found myself going back to it from time to time. Each time I would read a little more, and each time a seed was planted in me. I began to change on the inside.

My will began to line up with God's will. I was able to change areas in my life that needed to be changed. Changing on the outside pleases man, but it won't last. Changing on the inside pleases the Father and it *will* last. I began to meditate on Galatians 5:22, **But the fruit of the Spirit is love, joy, peace, longsuffering, gentleness, goodness, faith**. Then I allowed the fruit of the Spirit to grow in my life.

Also at this time, I was spending much time studying the Word, wanting to be a vessel pleasing to God and fit for His use. Therefore, being a doer of the Word included being a godly help meet. I began to line myself up according to the divine order of God for our household. We had a good marriage before, but now it is great! That doesn't mean our marriage is perfect, because people are not perfect. But our responsibility is to understand one another. Through the years, I have learned that most problems in a marriage arise from misunderstandings rather than selfishness.

When you walk in love and forgiveness, giving of yourself to one another, God will honor and bless your marriage.

Chapter Sixteen

I GREW UP IN A SINGING FAMILY

Make a joyful noise unto God, all ye lands: Sing forth the honour of his name: make his praise glorious.

Psalm 66:1-2

As far back as I can remember there was singing in our home. When we would travel in the car, we would sing together, each taking a particular part — either alto, tenor, soprano, lead, etc. It is funny now when I think about it, but I did not realize until I was grown and leading a children's choir that not everyone could sing parts. I just thought it came naturally.

Now we were not professionals by any means, even though mother and daddy did sing on the radio when they were younger. While we were growing up, my sisters and I sang in the church and for various functions around town. I remember one year my sister Shirley and I sang for the Miss Mississippi Pageant in Oxford, Mississippi, when we lived there.

By the time I got to high school, I was a soloist with the High School Swing Band and sang for school assemblies in Little Rock, Arkansas. I also sang on local television. I graduated with the senior distinction of "Most Talented." I was elated to have such an honor bestowed on me.

One time some men from Memphis, Tennessee, came to Little Rock. They wanted me to sign with them to make records. They were associated with the "Dot" label. You would think that a seventeen-year-old would jump at such a chance of a lifetime. But inside, I had a fear of doing that, probably for many different reasons.

However, the main reason I did not sign with them was that I felt God wanted me to sing for Him. During a revival meeting when I was fifteen years old, I dedicated my life to Him for "special service." I felt that my special service was, more than likely, singing. I did desire to be a preacher's wife until my girlfriend told me that it was probably the last thing I wanted! Her mother worked for a pastor and knew the pressures.

At any rate, the devil literally tried to destroy me for the next few years, and he almost did. There were times when it looked like he had! But praise God for His faithfulness. He never forgets our vows to Him. He took the rags of my life and made something beautiful of them. That's why I love Him so much.

When Happy got saved and the Lord called us into the ministry, it was like a dream come true. We traveled, sang, and Happy preached. I was serving God full-time. This was my special service. What joy filled my heart! I was so happy and content for the first time in many years.

On May 20, 1979, we started Agape Church. This was part of the vision the Lord had given us. In our church services, we have anointed praise and worship. We believe He should be lifted up and glorified above anything else.

One Sunday morning in 1982, Happy preached a message taken from Ezekiel 28:13-18 and Isaiah 14:11-26 about the fall of Lucifer. He was a master musician, anointed to lead praise and worship in heaven. He had been especially commissioned by God as the anointed cherub who covered, reflecting the glory of God with music in worship and praise.

The workmanship of thy tabrets (tambourines or percussion) **and of thy pipes** (all wind instruments) **was prepared in thee in the day that thou wast created** (Ez. 28:13b). He had the ability to create rhythm or a musical beat to music. In Isaiah 14:11, we see another series of instruments, **The noise of the viols...** Viols are six stringed instruments and thus could include all stringed instruments, such as the guitar and violin.

Lucifer was well able to lead praise and worship in heaven. When he fell, music fell with him. We now see Satan creating music by drawing praise and worship to himself, something he has always wanted. I was so grieved in my heart when I heard that message. I told God that I was willing to be an instrument of His praises, and I began to worship Him with everything that was in me.

As I yielded to the Lord, He told me not to be afraid of Him. He would not make me ashamed. Then the power of God hit me in the stomach and I doubled over. It felt like a ball of fire. The heat began to expand and permeate my body. An anointing came upon me. I really don't know how to explain it. From that day forward, I have worshiped Him faithfully in praise, worship, and song.

It had been a desire of my heart for many years to have a television program where I could sing and minister to hurting people.

The Lord opened the door for me to do that and now, during the weekly program, "In His Presence," I have the opportunity to minister to people who are oppressed of the devil and bound with all kinds of fears, sickness, and disease. I believe God will move by His Spirit to deliver each person who reaches out and receives deliverance. After all, He wants people to be free even more than they want it themselves.

I know that we should flow in the anointing God places on us, and that my first anointing is in singing and the second is in teaching. It took me a long time to accept the second anointing, but I will be happy doing what I am doing until Jesus comes. I started out in a singing family and will continue singing until I sing for Him face-to-face.

Chapter Seventeen

RECEIVE THE ANOINTING

The Spirit of the Lord is upon me, because he hath anointed me to preach the gospel to the poor; he hath sent me to heal the brokenhearted, to preach deliverance to the captives. . . .

Luke 4:18

I have told you how the Lord came upon me in a powerful way when I yielded to Him to be a vessel of praise and worship. A ball of fire hit me in the stomach and began to permeate throughout my body. Since that time, whenever I sing there has been an anointing to heal, deliver, refresh, and set the oppressed free. It is definitely a work of the Holy Spirit. I certainly cannot muster up an anointing, much less heal anybody.

Shortly after I first shared that experience in the *Agape Newsletter,* Buddy and Pat Harrison were at our church for a Holy Spirit Seminar. On the last night of the meeting, they called Happy and me and some of our associates up to minister to us by the Spirit. We were all blessed by what the Holy Spirit had to say to each of us. I was tremendously blessed because what the Lord said through Buddy lined up so beautifully with what I had written in the newsletter. I would like to share this Word with you. This is not intended to draw attention to me at all but to the anointing that God has placed on me when I minister in song. You could be the recipient of that anointing.

"Burn, burn, burn, for as you begin to sing, yes, it will begin to burn. Yes, as you begin to sing it will burn inside you and you will be able to see it full and clear, because that will help the flow of anointing and it will draw it near. For that will be the worship and the praise that will cause the blessings to come. But you will have your part to play and yes, the works of the enemy will be undone. For even as you have watched the birds in the backyard and seen the different colors in array, so you're going to see the move of the Holy Spirit the same way. Colorful, delightful, every size, every style, and every sound, and all of it is going to be in fullness and abound. So you'll see the Holy Spirit moving in His new dimension in this way, so get prepared for it because it will move on you and on your whole family and it will stay."

After the services, Buddy told me what he saw as he was giving me that word. He said, "There were bright colored lights, like the birds you watch, coming out of you and surrounding you. It was like flashes of it went out towards the people, and when they would receive it, the colors went into them."

Incidentally, I am a bird lover. I have bird feeders, birdhouses, bird books, and a bird water fountain in my back yard. I watch them from my kitchen window after I feed them, often with binoculars if I want a closer look. I could not begin to tell you all the species of birds I see every day — every color in the rainbow.

I was so excited about the word from the Lord regarding the colors that I began to meditate on it with my Bible. I started thinking, "When God spoke this earth into existence, it came with color. The grass and the trees are green; the fruit trees yield all kinds and colors of fruit; flowers and birds are a bouquet of color; the sky is blue — it goes on and on. Then I thought about the rainbow that is so absolutely beautiful with its arch of colors to thrill all our hearts. I looked in the Old Testament in Genesis 9:13 and read that God first placed the rainbow in the clouds as a covenant with Noah that He would never again cover the earth with water.

Then I thought about the rainbow that is in the New Testament in Revelation 4:3,5a. John described God sitting on His throne, and it was breathtaking. **And He that sat was to look upon like a jasper** (diamond) **and a sardine stone** (red)**: and there was a rainbow round about the throne, in sight like unto an emerald** (green)**. And out of the throne proceeded lightnings and thunderings and voices.** I believe the rainbow around the throne could be symbolic of God's covenant with Jesus Christ as head of the Church. Through this new covenant, we have available to us salvation, healing, deliverance, prosperity, love, joy, and peace.

I continued my search on rainbows and found Ezekiel 1:28. Ezekiel talks about the throne of God and the rainbow around it. He says the colors in the rainbow are the likeness of the glory of God. **As the appearance of the bow that is in the cloud in the day of rain, so was the appearance of the brightness round about. This was the appearance of the likeness of the glory of the Lord. And when I saw it, I fell upon my face, and I heard a voice of one that spake.**

Every time the Bible talks about the glory of God, there is always radiant, brilliant light. The glory is sometimes seen as a cloud, as fire, a bright light, or a rainbow. It is a special manifestation of His divine power and glory — the *Shekinah glory of God.*

I may be presumptuous and I could be wrong, but I believe what Buddy saw when he was giving me that word from the Lord was the *Shekinah glory* of the Lord flowing out to heal, deliver, and set His people free. I know that I don't have any power to heal, but *He* does, and I am willing to give myself to Him to be used for His glory.

Chapter Eighteen

A RESPECTER OF THE POOR

Seeing ye have purified your souls in obeying the truth through the Spirit unto unfeigned love of the brethren, see that ye love one another with a pure heart fervently.

1 Peter 1:22

It is amazing how the enemy of our soul works so hard to keep us in bondage by our thoughts. That is why the Bible has so much to say about renewing our minds or restoring our souls. Notice that you do not restore your spirit. Why? Because your spirit was born again. Your mind, however, has to be renewed or restored.

God wants our souls (mind, emotions, and will) to prosper with the abundance of the Word so we will know how to cast down vain or ungodly imaginations and bring every thought into obedience to Christ. (2 Cor. 10:5.) A wrong thought can become a stronghold, like a castle or fortress, in your mind and eventually run — and ruin — your life. Let me give you an example of a wrong thought that entered my mind early in our ministry. It caused me to walk in bondage in an area for about two years.

I have shared with you before how the devil told me that Happy and I had made a mistake in leaving our jobs and going into the ministry. He said, "How are you going to live?" The Lord took me to Matthew 6:24-33 and I found out that God would take care of us if we would always put Him first. From that day on, He has been the Source Who meets all our needs.

I came to realize that God uses *men* to bless us on this earth. According to Luke 6:38, **Give, and it shall be given unto you; good measure, pressed down, and shaken together, and running over, shall *men* give into your bosom. For with the same measure that ye mete withal it shall be measured to you again.** The deceptive thought the devil spoke to me was to avoid rich people, because they might think we were after their money.

I had observed a few unpleasant situations where ministers were puppets in the hands of rich benefactors, so I decided I would keep my distance. I did not have a problem with people who did not have money. I knew they would know we were not befriending them for their finances.

Let me say at this point that before we were in the ministry, I never had a problem with whether or not people had money. In fact, I had many wealthy friends. I also had middle-class friends and some that were poor. They were all the same to me. Their financial status was of no importance to me. I just liked them for who they were.

One day a minister and his wife came to town for a big crusade. While they were setting up, I was visiting with his wife. She said something like, "It seems that the poor people follow *our* ministry — not many wealthy people." I came to attention and said, "Well, we don't need the rich. The poor support us just fine." Her next statement then shot through me like an electrical shock, and it changed my thinking from that moment on. She said, "Yes, Jeanne, but we have to be careful not to be a *respecter of the poor.*" My heart was pierced by the Holy Spirit.

I thought with alarm, "I have been a respecter of the poor!" The Bible says that we are not to be a respecter of the rich, but God does not want us to be a respecter of the poor either. He does not want us to be a respecter of *persons, period.* In fact, Leviticus 19:15 says, **Ye shall do no unrighteousness in judgment: thou shalt not respect the person of the poor, nor honour the person of the mighty: but in righteousness shalt thou judge thy neighbour.**

I left that crusade a changed person on the inside. When I got home, I repented to the Lord for my wrong thinking and my wrong attitude. Rich people are God's people too. They can love Him just as much as anyone else can. Some of them work hard to obtain what they have in this life, while others are born with it — but it should not make any difference to us either way. I think many of us, at one time or another, have had wrong thoughts about the rich. The truth is, however, if it were not for the rich supporting the preaching of the gospel, I don't know where many ministries would be.

I am sure the offerings of the wealthy helped feed Jesus and His disciples many times as they labored to spread the gospel. We also find in Matthew 27:57 that a rich man named Joseph of Arimathaea gave his own tomb for Jesus' burial. In 2 John 1, John addresses the epistle to the "elect lady." *Elect lady* refers to a lady of means, who was well thought of in the church. So thank God for the rich as well as the poor.

We need to get our thinking in line with the Word of God. God, and not rich people, is still my source and always will be. However, I can honestly and gladly say that I am not a respecter of persons where money is concerned. The devil has lost yet another battle in my walk with God!

Chapter Nineteen

HIS PLAN FOR YOU

But seek ye first the kingdom of God, and his righteousness; and all these things shall be added unto you.

Matthew 6:33

When each new year rolls around, I know many of you set goals for yourself, your family, and your job or business. If you don't, you should. The Bible says, **Where there is no vision, the people perish: but he that keepeth the law, happy is he** (Prov. 29:18).

God has a plan for you in every new year. He will place that plan or vision in your heart like a seed, and then it is up to you to cause it to grow and come to pass. It is so rewarding to set goals and see them fulfilled. Success builds confidence in God and in yourself, and you need to accomplish your goals to maintain a good self-image.

You may ask, "How can I cause my vision or goals to come to pass?" First of all, set your goals and then don't be moved from them by any person or thing. You have to be firm. Do not be double-minded or tossed to and fro. Then begin speaking the Word of God over your goals. Your faith, expressed with the right words and followed by the appropriate actions, will cause them to come to pass, as long as they line up with the Word of God.

For instance, you may set a goal to prosper. However, if someone comes along and says, "It is not God's will for you to prosper," you drop your goal or vision. If you do that you will never prosper. Find some Scriptures to stand on and confess them daily. The Word will work if you will believe it and stand on it. Ask the Holy Spirit to keep you from error and He will.

You may set your goal to be a better wife or husband. One of the things you can do to meet that goal is to learn to be sensitive to your partner's needs. A self-centered partner will never know true happiness in a marriage.

You may set your goal to be a better mother or father. Take time to listen to your children. Spend quality time with them. Learn to control your temper by practicing patience. Remember, God is on your side! If you flub up, He will forgive you. But don't stop your confession or drop your goal.

Did you know that in Genesis 49:4 it says that Reuben would not excel because he was unstable? Therefore, in order for us to excel and fulfill our goals, we are going to have to be stable. Some of the definitions of *stable* are: "not likely to give way, firm, fixed, strong in character, purposeful, and steadfast." I like that.

I pray right now for *you* to set goals and be strong in character, have a purpose, and be steadfast and fixed in Jesus' name. I believe that you will continue to develop a close relationship with your Father God, and that you will spend time in prayer and reading the Word.

Make it your goal right now to be a success according to God's Word. You may rest assured that He wants this for you. He is your source! Seek Him and don't speak words that are contrary to the goals you have set. You will see them come to pass!

Chapter Twenty

THE BEST YEARS OF OUR LIVES

Let my mouth be filled with thy praise and with thy honour all the day.

Psalm 71:8

On Friday, February 11, 1972, at 11:05 p.m., in the old Ryman Auditorium in Nashville, Tennessee, my husband, Happy, was born again. It was the first broadcast of the "Grand Ole Gospel Time," which followed the famous "Grand Ole Opry." Rev. Jimmy Snow, son of the legendary Hank Snow, preached about ten minutes and Happy went forward to receive Jesus Christ as His Savior.

Prior to this time, Happy thought he *was* a Christian. He did not realize until that night that he was lost and had never made Jesus Christ the Lord and Savior of his life. He had been raised in a church that had given him a certificate when he was twelve years old stating that he agreed to accept Jesus Christ as his Savior. He knew

Jesus was the Son of God, but he had never accepted Him in his heart as Lord.

The weekend he was saved, we stayed in Nashville and attended Brother Snow's church on Sunday morning. It was a wonderful service, and we even had the privilege of seeing Johnny and June Cash there. That morning their chauffeur got saved! To this day, I can still see June Carter Cash on her knees beside him at the altar, her hands in the air and her coat thrown on the floor behind her. She was weeping with joy.

As we were flying back to Little Rock that afternoon, Happy looked at me and said, "Honey, I believe our life is going to change." Little did we know how much! One year later, we were in the ministry.

When we got home, the very first thing we did was start attending a home Bible study for a solid year. We were consumed with the precious Word of God and it completely changed our lives. You have already read about some of the ways I have been dramatically and forever changed.

After Happy had been saved a year, we went back to Nashville to celebrate the first anniversary of his salvation. Brother Snow had us sing that night on the "Grand Ole Gospel Time" program and Happy shared his testimony.

On February 11, 1992, Happy celebrated his twentieth year of salvation. Brother Snow called and asked if we would be his guests on the twentieth anniversary of the "Grand Ole Gospel Time" show. We were delighted to do so. We not only sang, but they had prepared a cake for Happy with balloons and everything. It was such a surprise! We never dreamed of such a thing. It was a joyous twentieth reunion for everyone.

I hope you have enjoyed me sharing Happy's testimony with you because *it is mine too.* What affects him affects me. God has been so gracious to us over the last 20 years. It has been a *joy* to serve Him. Although I hope He does not delay His coming for another twenty years, if He does, we will just have to go back to Nashville and have another celebration!

Chapter Twenty-One

THE CHURCH AS A WHOLE

There is one body, and one Spirit, even as ye are called in one hope of your calling; One Lord, one faith, one baptism, One God and Father of all, who is above all, and through all, and in you all.

Ephesians 4:4-6

A few years ago, Happy and I went to Sri Lanka with Deo and Elaine Miller, who are part of our missionary outreach at Agape Church. Sri Lanka is a small, tear-shaped island right at the tip of India. It is a war-torn, poverty-stricken country in constant religious turmoil between the Tamils, who are Hindus, and the Singhalese, who are Buddhist. Christianity is almost nonexistent. However, the numbers of Christians are growing, thanks to the men and women of faith who have given their very lives for the cause of Christ.

Some of the things I saw in Sri Lanka pricked my heart and left a scar that will be with me forever. A scar is a mark that is left after a wound. I was indeed wounded by the large statues of Buddha that

I saw every mile that we drove. Some of them were almost three stories high. By contrast, in America you see a church every mile and take it for granted. Even our coins say, "In God We Trust." We are a *Christian nation*, regardless of our faults.

When I returned home, I saw the Church as a *whole* more than ever before. It really does not matter what our differences are. As long as Jesus Christ is Lord and we are born again, we are members of His Body. In America you can go one mile and see a Baptist church; go another mile and see an Assemblies of God church; and go another mile and see a Faith church, to name a few. Although there are differences, each church represents Jesus Christ — not a statue of Buddha, a dumb idol representing a false god.

If we Christians could only get a revelation of the "Church as a whole" and start pulling together for the cause of Christ, how this would please our Father God! We all need each other. We are brothers and sisters in Christ and we should love one another. You may think you don't need another's love, but you do. There may be someone at another church whom God may use to give you a word of wisdom when you are in trouble, or confirm something He has told you to do.

This happened to me in October of 1983, in the incident I related in the preface of this book. The Lord spoke to me to start teaching a ladies' Bible study, but the day before I was to teach, I was wondering if I had really heard from God correctly. About that time a preacher in another state, whom Happy and I had not talked to in years, called to tell me of a dream he had had about me. He said he saw me teaching people how to be mature Christians and that what I was doing was very important. His call was confirmation to me and it brought peace and confidence that God was directing my footsteps.

We need to pray that our attitudes will be like Jesus'— to love one another and serve one another unselfishly, regardless of our differences. There should be no competition or jealousy among us. I don't believe we will ever come together in our doctrine, but we can come together in our faith. What we *believe* may divide us, but *Who* we believe in unites us. I realize people teach things that I do not agree with at all. But I can still love them because they are a part of Christ's body, the Church. We need to endeavor to strengthen one another.

A while back, I heard award-winning vocalist Steve Green on television. He was saying that a song he recorded had been very controversial. The song is called, "Let the Walls Come Down." He sang the song and it was powerful. The chorus goes:

> *Let the walls come down that divide us,*
> *Let the walls come down that hide us,*
> *If in Christ we agree, let us seek unity,*
> *Let the walls come down.*

Steve said he thought the unity of the Church was a mandate of Christ. Amen and amen!

Chapter Twenty-Two

ERUPTION, DESTRUCTION, OR CONSTRUCTION?

Being confident of this very thing, that he which hath begun a good work in you will perform it until the day of Jesus Christ.

Philippians 1:6

In the fall of 1978, the Lord spoke to Happy to raise up a church in Little Rock. When Happy told me what the Lord had said, I told him that he had been eating too much garlic! Even the very thought of being pastors of a church caused me to almost have night- mares. Let me explain that statement by going back to the beginning of our ministry.

In February of 1972, after Happy got saved, the first thing he did was join the choir at the church we were attending. Shortly afterwards we were asked to sing a special in the Sunday service. That seemingly ordinary event actually started us into the full-time ministry of gospel singing. From that point on we were asked to sing in churches all over Arkansas and a number of other states.

In March of 1973 we recorded our first album in Nashville as the "Agape Singers." In the fall of 1973 we were guests on "The 700 Club" in Virginia, where we sang most of the songs from our new album. We were thrilled beyond words!

We continued traveling and singing all over the United States and in March, 1974, Happy began teaching the Word. God was moving powerfully in our services and in our lives. Everything was wonderful until the Lord spoke to Happy to take over the pastorate of a local church that he had helped raise up. The previous pastor had felt led to go into full-time evangelism. The Lord told Happy to pastor for a season, so that is what we did during 1975 and 1976.

The church doubled in size from 200 to 400 people while we were there. We had some wonderful, life-changing experiences and met some precious people there. But we also had some very difficult, hurtful experiences. For instance, one day a lady came in and told us that she had hate in her heart for us and wanted us to forgive her. Of course we did, but we sat and licked our wounds after she left. Hated us? What had we done to her? We were just trying to obey God.

The very next week, another lady came in and said the same thing. When she left, we just looked at each other and said, "Well, what else is new?" Come to find out, they belonged to a prayer group that thought their leader, who was a minister, should have become the new pastor instead of Happy.

Our season was up, and by 1977 we were once again on the road, singing and teaching the Word. How refreshing it was! You see, we were a family — Happy, our son Ronnie, and me — and were always together. We used to try and figure out why in the world God wanted us to pastor a church for a season. We decided it was to help us understand the role of a pastor so we could work better with them in their churches.

Almost two years later, when the Lord spoke to Happy to raise up a church in Little Rock, I was aghast! Many churches in Little Rock had been through all kinds of strife and splits. I felt like the last thing Little Rock needed was another church. Therefore, we put the idea of pastoring a church on the shelf for awhile.

In February of 1979 we were part of a campmeeting in California, along with Buddy and Pat Harrison. After the meeting, we all took our kids to an amusement park to enjoy the day. That morning, as we were having breakfast, Happy asked me if he could share with them what the Lord had said to him about raising up a church in Little Rock. I said, "You might as well."

As he began to share with them, the Holy Spirit came over us like a big cloud. It seemed as if we were the only people in the restaurant, even though it was packed. I began to bawl like a baby, telling them about the poor people in Little Rock who had been so hurt from all the splits. I did not know I even cared!

Pat Harrison began to speak in tongues and Buddy interpreted saying, "Go back home and find a place to start a church. Start where you are." Later, I was talking to Buddy and said, "You just don't know the eruption that will take place when we go back and start a new church." He turned to me and said, *"The eruption that will come will not be one of destruction but construction to build the body of Christ."*

So in May of 1979 we started Agape Church. I can honestly say with all my heart that this church has been the most exciting, most blessed, most rewarding experience of our lives. We had learned much from our last pastorate and soon came to look on the "pastor for a season" experience as wonderful schooling to prepare us for Agape Church.

Agape continues to reach out to our city, state, nation, and world through Agape Academy (a church school) and Agape School of World Evangelism and Laymen's School, where we send missionaries all around the world; and through Christian radio and television stations reaching our city and state. We have "Kids Like You," a team that ministers on television throughout the United States and Africa, and travels in other countries holding children's services. Special seminars and ministry go on every week at the church. We are, by the help of the Holy Spirit, *"building the body of Christ,"* just as God said.

Obeying God is the most important thing you can do in life, although it is not always easy. He will bless you and see you through all kinds of situations, though sometimes you might think He has forgotten you are alive! But through it all, I have always found Him to be a faithful Father.

Chapter Twenty-Three
NO WAY

When the even [evening] was come, they brought unto him many that were possessed with devils [demons]: and he cast out the spirits with his word, and healed all that were sick.

Matthew 8:16

It is so beautiful how the Lord equips you to do what He calls you to do. I never thought I would see the day when I would cast a demon out of someone, but the day came and there have been many others since then.

When I was a small child, folks did not have television to occupy their time, so they would sit around and tell ghost stories. I remember being deathly afraid of ghosts. Many nights, I would cover my head so they could not get me! As I grew older, I realized there was no such thing as ghosts, but even so, I still had a fear of the unknown.

After Happy got saved and we began to study the Bible, I learned there *were* demon spirits. Then I *really* got scared, because I realized something *was* out there trying to get me. When we first went into the ministry and I heard stories about people casting out demons, I would think, "No way! I will never do anything like that!" I was serious about it too. Like I said, I was very afraid of the unknown.

From time to time I would hear someone preach a sermon about demons and would plug my ears. I did not want to hear about it. When one day the Lord told me He wanted me to learn all about evil spirits because He wanted to use me to cast them out, I just acted like I did not hear Him. But He was persistent!

The Holy Spirit directed me to three books on demons by Kenneth E. Hagin. They taught that a believer has authority over these evil spirits. I bought them and prepared myself to read and learn. When I first began reading, I was petrified to realize demon spirits were for real. I kept looking around to make sure one would not get me. But as I continued to read, I saw the authority we have in the Name of Jesus and by His blood. I found out they were actually afraid of me — a believer! When I found out the truth, it set me free. How exciting it was to find out that Satan had been stripped of his authority and he and his demons had to bow their knee to the name of Jesus.

Before too long, I realized the authority I had over the devil when the Lord sent a demon-possessed nineteen-year-old girl to see Happy and me. She had been baptized into the Church of Satan and was trying to get free from its members, but could not. They had a curse on her that if she tried to leave, they would kill her.

When we laid hands on her, she jumped out of the chair she was sitting in, knocking it over. She pushed a desk sideways and knocked the pencil sharpener off the wall. I mean she was getting out of there! I perceived that if she got away, Satan would try to kill her. I yelled, "Stop in the Name of Jesus." She stopped suddenly and stood like a wooden soldier. She could not move.

Happy and I then began to cast the demon spirits out of her. They came out one by one and she was set free by the power of Almighty God. I can still remember the tears running down her cheeks as she confessed Jesus as her Lord. I thanked God for teaching me about deliverance and then giving me the opportunity to see this girl set free. What a blessing it was! It so touched my heart.

Casting out demons is a part of the ministry of Jesus, just as healing is. He came to set His people free. If you are interested, more than any other book in the New Testament, the Book of Mark gives insight into this area of Jesus' ministry.

Since that day, we have ministered to hundreds of people and seen them set free. I am no longer afraid of the devil or his demons. Thanks be to God for His Word that teaches us the authority we have as Christians!

In this day and hour we need to know what to do when we discern the presence of a demon. Then we can help those who have been deceived by the enemy. God help us all to be mighty warriors, defeating evil in Jesus' name!

Chapter Twenty-Four

PEACE AND JOY — THE CHOICE IS YOURS

And if it seem evil unto you to serve the Lord, choose you this day whom ye will serve.

Joshua 24:15

God has made us free moral agents with the privilege of making choices. During the holidays, many people surrender to the stress and pressures that seem to come with buying gifts and entertaining family and friends; however, they can choose to make any holiday season — or any season at all — a joyous time. You can make the decision to have a blessed, peaceful, and joyful time no matter what. Although the situation may not appear to be peaceful or even blessed, you can be in your heart and attitude. The choice is yours!

As Christians, we have made the decision to follow God. But have we made the decision to follow Him as Jesus did? Are we following Him in complete submission to His will? We are the result of all the choices we make in our lives. If we don't like the decisions we have made, we can't blame God. The good news is that we can choose to change them today.

It is your choice to be either negative or positive, happy or sad, mad or glad, haughty or humble, hateful or grateful. If you will just *choose* to let Jesus express Himself through you, you will experience peace and joy — not just during the holidays, but throughout the year. Let Jesus talk through you, love through you, give through you, and heal through you. In this way, you can influence others to have peace and joy as well.

It is not always easy to choose God's way, but His way always proves to be the best. The key is to walk in the Spirit and constantly put down the flesh and any offenses that come. I told Happy one day, "You know, it is easier to grow up physically than it is spiritually." Oh sure, there are problems with growing up physically, but the problems we encounter in our spiritual growth can cause us to stumble and fall short of the things of God.

In Galatians 5:19-26 we see the difference between walking in the flesh and walking in the Spirit. You might say, "Dear me, I'm not going to murder anyone or get drunk or commit adultery." But what about strife? Hatred? Envy? Variance and discord? Offenses? Resentment? Crucifying the flesh in these areas is often much harder! As Christians we are to strive to walk in the Spirit and crucify the flesh. It is possible to be a mature Christian in these areas, because God would not tell us to do something if we could not do it!

One way to walk in the Spirit is to pray in the Spirit. That will bring your soul and body into subjection to your spirit. Then you will know the mind of God as He brings His thoughts to you. You will know what to say and how to act as you look to Him, and His power and love will help you choose peace in every situation. Psalm 37:23 says, **The steps of a good man are ordered by the Lord: and he delighteth in his way.** He will give you the ability to say, "My God is able and so am I."

One day when I was teaching a ladies Bible study, I taught how we can find more excuses for why *other* people are happy. Have you ever said, "Sure they are happy. They are rich." Or, "Of course they are happy, they have children." Or, "I would be happy too if my spouse went to church with me." Yet true happiness and joy come from God, the all-sufficient One as you make the moment-by-moment decisions to trust Him. He is your joy, for He is love and He is life.

Make the choice to look to Him and you will be blessed during every holiday season and the entire year!

Chapter Twenty-Five

IT'S A SMALL WORLD

With God all things are possible.

Matthew 19:26b

While I was still in bed one morning in April of 1989, I was looking at the ceiling above me when I had an open vision. All of a sudden the earth came from my right side and hovered over me about six feet in the air. It was about the size of a basketball. It stayed there for about five seconds, then moved to my left out of sight.

Suddenly the globe came around again and stopped right before my eyes for another five seconds; then it left again. The third time it came into my view, the United States became very clear, as if it had been outlined. While I was looking at it, the state of Arkansas became very bold and bright, and then a hand reached out from it. The palm was towards me and the five fingers were extending and expanding in different directions around the earth. Then it left.

I leaped out of bed and bounded into the kitchen where Happy was making some fresh orange juice. I could not talk fast enough because I was so excited about what I had just seen. Happy just looked at me and all I heard was, "Huh?" We were both wondering what it could possibly mean.

I was impacted with the feeling that this world is really very small and that we *can* reach it for Christ. I also felt strongly that for most people the world is only as large as the place they live. For others, it might be as big as the places they have traveled to in their state or within the United States. Still others have been around the world. In any case, each has had the experience of saying, "It's a small world, isn't it?"

Two years ago when Happy and I went to Singapore for an ICFM Ministers Convention, we went downtown with another couple to do some shopping. While we were shopping, some people overheard us talking and asked, "What part of the South are you from?" When we told them we were from Arkansas, they said, "Arkansas! We are from Benton, Arkansas." I said to them, "Our office manager is from Benton. Do you happen to know Libby Bailey?" They said, "Yes, we went to school together." If you don't think the world is small, think again!

I was teaching the ladies Bible study the morning I had the vision, so I shared it with them. I also went to see Kim Nance, the administrator of Agape School of World Evangelism, and told her about the vision. She later had "Reaching Out to the World" printed on the cover of the ASWE brochure.

I got a world globe and began to study it with great excitement, seeing where I had been and where I would like to go. I started visualizing all the oceans dried up and saw the continents coming together like a puzzle. The Bible says that one day they will be dried up, according to Revelation 21:1, **...and there was no more sea.**

In May, during our annual Spring Campmeeting, the children of Agape Academy presented me with a globe they had made with little paper hands reaching out to the world. Everyone was excited about the vision!

When I had the vision in 1989, seeing the world like that was a little unusual. But now everywhere you look you see something about the world in some form or fashion. You see it on T-shirts, coffee cups, magazines, televisions, and books. We see all kinds of programs about saving the planet by encouraging actions such as recycling. Ministers of the gospel are talking about going into all the world to save the lost. People in general have become world-minded. A one-world currency seems to be a reality in the near future, and the Bible tells us we are headed for a one-world government.

There is no doubt about it. We are headed for a change — a big change! Things are beginning to line up for the Rapture of the Church and for the antichrist to rise to power afterward. When he does, the next seven years on this earth will be a different era indeed. During the first three and a half years there will seemingly be peace, but the next three and a half years will be absolutely dreadful.

For then shall be great tribulation, such as was not since the beginning of the world to this time, no, nor ever shall be.
Matthew 24:21

What a horrible thought! It is really hard to even imagine. But it is coming and coming sooner than we think. Folks, we must reach the world for Christ! In the past few years we have seen doors of utterance open like never before. People are hearing the gospel for the very first time and are eagerly accepting Jesus as their Lord. The harvest is truly white and ripe. We *must* do what God has called each one of us to do.

It is time for the church to reach the world, and God has a plan for *you*! Each of us has a purpose and plan for our lives. We are each unique — no two people are alike. Isn't that remarkable? And each of us has a vision that the Lord has placed in our hearts and in our minds. Let us reach out, take it, and fulfill it!

You may ask, "How can I know for sure that what is in my thoughts is from God?" First and foremost, *ask* God to make it clear to you. Spend time with Him in prayer and reading His Word so that you will know His thoughts and His will. All you have to do is line up your thoughts and your will to His. It is His desire and plan to change you and use you for His glory.

During the coming days, I challenge you to step out and do what God has commanded. Walk in your calling and gifts with great boldness and love to reach the whole world with the good news of Jesus Christ!

Chapter Twenty-Six

THANK YOU, LORD, FOR MY NEW KIRBY

Now faith is the substance of things hoped for, the evidence of things not seen.

Hebrews 11:1

The Lord has impressed me to include the following testimony to encourage you in your walk of faith. If you are believing God for something and it has not yet been manifested, I believe this word will increase your faith and give you strength and hope.

Several years ago on a sunny afternoon, I was cleaning my house when someone knocked on the door. It was a Kirby vacuum cleaner salesman. Having so much to do, I would have turned him away, but he offered to shampoo the carpet in one room for free if I would allow him a demonstration. I agreed! He cleaned the rug and showed me all the many ways this vacuum cleaner would benefit me and my carpets. I really wanted one, but it was more than I felt I could pay at the time. I told him, "I will get one — but not today."

After he left, I asked the Lord for one. I said, "Lord, this is not a selfish prayer. I need a new vacuum cleaner very badly. I ask you to give me a new Kirby in the Name of Jesus and I receive it now." *I knew in my heart that I had one,* but I did not know *how* I was going to get it. I thought maybe the Lord would give me the money. All I knew was that I *would have* one.

Every few weeks the young man from Kirby called me and asked if I was ready to buy the vacuum cleaner. I told him, "Not yet, but I am going to get one." Finally, after a while, he quit calling. Still, I did not quit thanking the Lord for it. Every time I would use my vacuum cleaner, I would say, "Thank You, Lord, for my new Kirby."

Now it is in the waiting that many people give up and stop believing. I went for months saying, "Thank You, Lord, for my new Kirby." I did not nag Him about it. I did not fall down and cry, "Why didn't you give me a Kirby. I thought You would." No, I just thanked Him every time I vacuumed.

Several months later, Happy was conducting a radio "Talk-A-Thon" at a hotel in Little Rock. We were praying for the needs of the people in the listening audience and having a great time in the Lord. Our friends were answering the phones, taking prayer requests, and receiving new partners into the radio ministry. We also had cake, coffee, and a copy of our latest record release, "Country Cajun Chorus," for all who came by to see us.

A young man wandered in. I welcomed him, gave him a record, and told him to make himself at home. Then I received a call so I went to the phones. When I got off the phone, he looked at me and said, "I have something to give you." I said, "Well, praise God," supposing it was a donation into the radio ministry. I said, "What is it?" He said, "A vacuum cleaner." When he said that, my mind went immediately to the day I asked the Lord for the vacuum cleaner. I thought, "Lord, could this possibly be my Kirby?" I felt like my heart was going to explode. With trembling lips and tearful eyes, I asked, "What kind?" He paused for a moment and said, "A Kirby."

Needless to say, I had my own campmeeting right there! I took three giant steps toward him and hugged him. I was so excited, I could not hold back the tears. Everyone looked at me with wonder and amazement. They did not know what was going on inside of me. Only my Jesus knew. Let me say at this point that I had not told anyone about my request to the Father — not Happy, not a friend, no one — just God, my Father who is my source. Also, the Kirby vacuum cleaner man was *not* the same man who had come by my house earlier. The man in the studio was a spirit-filled Christian, led there by the Holy Spirit.

The young salesman got excited because I was so excited! He ran out to his car, brought the Kirby in, and assembled it there before everybody. I asked him how he came about giving me a vacuum cleaner. He said he was driving around town making sales calls and listening to our live broadcast. Suddenly the Spirit of the Lord said to him, "You have been saying with your mouth that if you give, God will return your giving one hundred-fold. If you really believe that, I want you to give those folks on the air a vacuum cleaner." This young salesman needed to increase his sales, so he quickly obeyed!

What makes this story even better is that he had two vacuum cleaners in the trunk of his car. One was a Kirby, the other an Electrolux. I have nothing against Electrolux, I just happened to have asked for a Kirby. Anyway, he said he did not know which one he was going to give me when he came into the studio and did not know until I asked him. He said the only thing that came to him was the Kirby vacuum cleaner! Praise God, I received exactly what I asked Him for. He is faithful to His Word! And incidentally, that very same day the young man received an order in the mail for a new vacuum cleaner. Praise God for His faithfulness!

Chapter Twenty-Seven

MY PEOPLE NEED TO LAUGH

The joy of the Lord is your strength.

Nehemiah 8:10b

❧

Every spring we hold an event for the ladies of our church called "Ladies Advance." This is a time to get away for a couple of days and get relaxed, refreshed, and renewed in spirit, soul, and body.

During a recent Advance, the Lord had me teach on laughter. He said, "My people need to laugh." There are so many terrible things going on in the world today. If Christians don't watch out, we will fall into the same depression that afflicts the world. We may be *in* the world, but we are not *of* the world, and Jesus wants us to have joy. (John 17:13.)

Proverbs 17:22 says, **A merry heart doeth good like a medicine: but a broken spirit drieth the bones.** What does medicine do for you? It assists your body in healing. Laughter does this too. It is good like a medicine. It provides a marvelous resistance against disease in the body, unhappiness in the home, and strife in the church. Now you can't beat that!

Medical science now acknowledges that the best resistance against disease is laughter. They define laughter as "stationary jogging," because the muscles and blood pressure react in such a healthy way during laughter. After laughing, the body benefits from its relaxed state.

I recently saw Dr. Annette Goodheart, a clinical psychiatrist who conducts "laugh therapy," on Christian television. She said the physical advantages from laughter are amazing. It affects the heart and digestive system and enhances the immune system's ability to fight off diseases like a preventive medicine.

Laughter releases chemicals called endorphins into the body. "Endorphin" is a combination of two words: endogenous, which means something produced within, and morphine, which is a medication for pain control and relaxation. Because of His love for us, God has placed in His Word verses about us having joy. Joy produces the very chemical in our body that will help us calm down and stop pain. Like morphine that is administered from an external source, joy and laughter release endorphins within our body's unique system, designed exactly as God intended. If we laugh just 20 minutes a day, our body releases enough endorphins to keep us healthy and happy. Praise God!

When you need to laugh, just "fake it 'til you make it." Your diaphragm does not know the difference and you will receive the same benefits. When you put sound to a merry heart, it comes out as laughter. Laughter is joy overflowing! However, it does take a conscious effort to have a merry heart.

Joy is a fruit of your recreated spirit, but it has to be cultivated.

Philippians 4:4 says, **Rejoice in the Lord always: and again I say, Rejoice.** It does not say to rejoice *sometimes!* If you are having trouble rejoicing, begin to speak the Word that will build you up and put on some good Christian music that will fill your heart with joy. Dance before the Lord in praise and adoration. Think of all the wonderful things God has done for you. Fellowship with the Father and let Him love you, because knowing He loves you will bring joy.

Dr. Goodheart pointed out that we take ourselves too seriously. As children we were often not allowed to laugh, and as adults we are told not to laugh or people will not take us seriously. We can free ourselves from a lot of heavy burdens if we learn to laugh at ourselves, as well as with others. Remember too that self-pity will be your downfall as it was Israel's. They wished they had died in the wilderness and they did! Don't allow self-pity into your life.

Many Christians do experience depression. Depression means low spirits, gloominess, dejection, sadness, and a decrease in strength. Almost everyone has experienced depression at one time or another, but some folks enjoy pity parties. They spread their gloom and despair everywhere they go. They need to recognize the enemy, resist him (James 4:7) and then begin thinking positive thoughts and speaking positive words. Put on **the garment of praise for the spirit of heaviness** (Is. 61:3).

The Ladies Advance was a tremendous success. Many ladies returned home set free from of all kinds of bondage. Others, like me, came home refreshed and blessed. So my message to you is this: Don't take yourself too seriously! Learn to laugh at yourself and with others. And, learn to enjoy life and have fun!

Chapter Twenty-Eight

CONTENTMENT

Not that I speak in respect of want: for I have learned, in what-soever state I am, therewith to be content.

Philippians 4:11

I remember very vividly when the Lord impacted me with the above Scripture. It was 1974 in the home of Mr. and Mrs. Ken Wanty, who lived in Michigan. I would like to share the story in hopes that it will help you.

In the first few years of our ministry, we traveled in a van all across America. We dearly loved what we were doing and did not want to do anything else. God was using us to minister to people through singing and teaching the Word, and the Lord opened doors for us to minister in many churches.

When we ministered, we had to stay in the homes of church people or the pastor, as they usually did not put us in a hotel. Although many times the people were wonderful, there were other times when we were not wanted and felt they just endured us for the day or two we were with them.

One time we drove up to a pastor's home, where we were to stay while ministering to his church. When his wife opened the door she said, "Oh, it's you. I didn't think you were coming." Happy told her our meeting had been confirmed for some time and that we had driven all day in order to make it. (We would have gladly stayed in a motel, but there were none in that little town.)

She half-heartedly invited us in but let us know very quickly that she was not well and was not up to doing anything. That was easy to see. Every dish was dirty and stacked on the kitchen counter. There was no food in the refrigerator, and the house looked like a tornado had just blown through.

 Before her husband came home, I washed all the dishes and started cleaning her house. When her husband arrived he fixed dinner, and I washed the dishes again. I hurriedly dressed for church that night, ministered, and then came home exhausted. I went to bed, and we left early the next morning for our next meeting.

Something similar happened when we were on a three-week tour through Kentucky, Ohio, and Michigan. The couple with whom we stayed in Kentucky was not on speaking terms. The wife complained to me all day and half the night for three days. I did not get much rest at all. I also cleaned and cooked there. When we left, I was physically, mentally, and spiritually drained.

I told Happy, "When we get to Michigan, I am not staying with another person. I want to stay in a motel." He said, "There is not much we can do about it if they have already made arrangements for us to stay with someone." But my mind was made up. I had *had* it.

When we arrived at our destination, you might know they had us staying with a "wonderful family." I thought, "Yeah, sure." On the way to the house, I told Happy that although I might have to go, I was not going to be nice.

When we arrived, the Wantys met us with big, warm smiles. I got out of the van, asked where we would be staying, and went straight to our room and shut the door. I laid down across the bed to rest awhile and opened my Bible to read. I turned to the Book of Philippians and began reading. All at once, I came to Philippians 4:11. When I read that verse, it was as if it jumped right off the page and into my heart.

I was so convicted by the Holy Spirit for my childish un-Christlike behavior. Immediately I got on my knees beside the bed and asked the Lord to forgive me for not being content in whatsoever state I was in. After praying I got up, washed my face, and went into the den to visit with the family.

I want you to know that this family was absolutely beautiful in every way. Mrs. Wanty did not let me lift a finger. She had all the meals prepared beforehand and would not allow me to set the table or wash a dish. She said, "You came to minister to us and we want to minister to you." Isn't that just like God to bless us when we really need it?

I had determined to let the love of God flow through me no matter what the situation, but the Wantys were easy to love. God's love flowed through them to us.

The Scripture says, "For I have learned" (or experienced). All of us have had experiences, but did we learn from them? The key to a life that is free from agitation and strife is *learning* to be content, no matter what your circumstances are. Webster's Dictionary defines contentment as "uncomplaining acceptance of one's position."

Let the peace of God rule in your heart. (Col. 3:15.) Get rid of self-pity and depression and choose to be happy. Endeavor to create an environment of peace. Set aside a time and place to be calm — a place where there are no distractions or interruptions. Read the Bible and let the Word of God minister peace to you. Make up your mind to be content in every situation!

Chapter Twenty-Nine

PUT THE BLAME
WHERE IT BELONGS

My son, forget not my law; but let thine heart keep my commandments: For length of days, and long life, and peace, shall they add to thee.

Proverbs 3:1-2

Recently Happy and I went to Branson, Missouri, for a few days of recreation and fun with a group of friends. We had a wonderful time. While there, we had the privilege of meeting Barbara Mandrell and her husband, Ken. She is a Christian and a very delightful person. She gave us a copy of her book, *Get To The Heart*. In it, she shares her life story and goes into great detail about the tragic automobile accident she had in 1984.

While reading the book, I came across something that really got my attention. I found myself thinking about it from time to time. In fact, I read it to Happy and shared my thoughts with him. The more I thought on it, the more I wanted to share it with you. It may help you now, the way it *could* have helped me years ago.

Barbara told about a car wreck she was in when she was eighteen years old. She also said that about the same time her dog was killed by a car. So she went to talk to a minister because she was very depressed. She wanted to know, "Why does God do these things?" The minister told her, "It was not God's fault. He did not do this." He said, "You knew the car tires were slick but you did not have them changed, and you were the one who left the gate open so that the dog got out." He continued, "God doesn't do bad things."

She said his remarks gave her such peace and brought her to her senses. "I was blaming my heavenly Father, but I found out that *I* had messed up." Therefore, years later when she was in a terrible automobile accident where she was badly hurt, she did not blame God.

When I read this story I couldn't believe my eyes. You hardly ever hear of a minister talking like that about God. They usually say something religious like, "Well, it was God's will" or, if someone dies, "God needed them in heaven."

As I related in chapter 7, when I lost my daddy as a child, the very first thing my pastor said to me was, "God took your daddy because He needed him in heaven." What an awful thing to say to a child who had just lost the dearest person in her life! And what a terrible thing to say to a young mother who had little girls to raise by herself.

Unfortunately, his statement about God caused me to live many years not loving my heavenly Father. How could you love someone who killed your daddy? I blamed every bad thing that happened to me on God. I did not trust Him. I thought, "You just never know what He might do to you." I served God strictly out of fear, not love.

It was years later that I found out the truth about God. I found out that He was a lover, not a killer. He came to give us life, not death. He is for us, not against us. He is a good God, not evil. He does good things. His desire is for us to live long and be satisfied. What joy and peace it brought to me when I got a revelation of God, my Father. He *is* my Father, my dearest Friend, the Lord of my Life. I can *trust* him.

If I had been told by my pastor what Barbara was told by her minister, my life would have been different. (Today, if I would allow it, I could be angry just thinking about it!) One thing I certainly did learn from reading Barbara's book is how *responsible* we are for what we say to people about God.

We can ruin someone's thinking and life with the wrong words about God. It would be better to say, "I don't know the answer," than to say something that is a lie and contrary to the Word of God.

Psalm 91:16 says, **With long life will I satisfy him, and shew him my salvation.** Proverbs 9:11 says, **For by me thy days shall be multiplied, and the years of thy life shall be increased.** We also find in John 10:10 that, **The thief** [the devil] **cometh not, but for to steal, and to kill, and to destroy: I** [Jesus] **am come that they might have life, and that they might have it more abundantly.**

Believe me, you can depend on God. Just because you don't understand why something happened or did not happen, don't blame God. *Put the blame where it belongs.* Pray and ask Him to reveal the truth of the matter to you, and He will. He will never fail you! Remember, He is for you, not against you, because you are His child and He loves you.

Chapter Thirty

I WILL TAKE HEED TO MY WAYS

Death and life are in the power of the tongue: and they that love it shall eat the fruit thereof.

Proverbs 18:21

The Bible has so much to say about the use of our tongue. We can minister life, love, and peace with our tongue, or we can let the devil use it to steal, kill, and destroy. I remember very clearly when the Lord spoke to me about my tongue.

In 1973 our family went to Texarkana to minister in song at a church. After the services were over, a group of people went out to eat and have fellowship. I tried very hard to get along with everybody, but I felt like I was missing it somewhere. So, before going to sleep that night, I asked the Lord to help me know what to do.

Before daylight the next morning, I awoke suddenly with a thought, "Read Psalm 39." I knew in my heart God was about to tell me something. So as not to wake Happy, I went to the bathroom with my Bible, closed the door, and turned on the light. I quickly turned to Psalm 39 and began reading verse 1. It said, **I will take heed to my ways, that I sin not with my tongue: I will keep my mouth with a bridle, while the wicked is before me.**

The Lord wanted me to adhere to the first part and take heed to my ways by keeping my mouth shut, no matter who was before me. I thanked Him for showing me what steps to take to get along with people.

You see, up to this time in my life, I had a very sharp tongue and could "hold my own" with the very best of them. I had worked in the secular world for many years and had learned to take care of myself! After all, I thought that if I didn't, nobody else would. I was also very opinionated and would give you my opinion whether you asked for it or not. You can see I had my work cut out for me! But praise God for the Holy Spirit. I did not have to do it alone.

At that time, I was still working in an office downtown. I typed Psalm 39:1 on a strip of paper and put it on my file box so I could see it all the time. It was a constant reminder for me to "bridle my tongue." There were so many times I wanted to talk about the boss when he was gone, give my opinion, or straighten someone out. But I would see that Scripture and hold my tongue. I was learning to take heed to my ways.

Over the next few months, it became easier and easier to bridle my tongue at the office. But the Lord also wanted me to bridle my tongue at home with my husband and son, at church, and at Bible study. He wanted it to be a *lifestyle,* not just an occasional thing. I diligently worked at accomplishing this goal, because God was doing this for *my* benefit. He was answering *my* prayer.

The Holy Spirit was helping me, but you must always remember that the only way He can help you is for you to stay in the Word of God. You have to abide in Him and He will abide in you. (John 15:4.) When you read the Word, it gets down into your heart, and Jesus said, **for out of the abundance of the heart the mouth speaketh** (Matt. 12:34).

If you will do just a little study on the tongue, you will see how powerful it really is. Your concordance will refer you to Scriptures about your lips or your words. Take the time to look them up and meditate on them. They will bless and help you.

By taking heed to my own ways — what I say, how I say it, and when I say it — and by learning to be a *listener* instead of always *talking*, my ways have become prosperous in the Lord. People need to know you care about them. Talking is sharing, but listening is caring. As you apply this principle in your life, I know that your ways will become prosperous too!

the Holy Spirit is helping me. Jesus said, "I have told you
that the only way He can help you is for you to stay in the Word of
God. You have to abide in Him and He will abide in you. (John
17:4) When you read the Word... it goes down into your heart, and
issues out for out of the abundance of the heart a man the mouth
speaketh (Mat. 12:34)."

It you will do just a little study of the tongue, you will see how
powerful it really is. Your concordance will help you to see how great
about your thoughts or words. Read the things about them again and
meditate on them. They will bless and help you.

By paying heed to our own ways — what I say, how I say it, and
when I say it — and by learning to be a disquieter of errant talk,
say to yourself the more profitable, from in the Lord. Learn to yield to
know your rate about them. Talking is sharing, but listening is caring. As you apply this principle in your life, I know that your ways
will become pleasing too.

Chapter Thirty-One

MY MOTHER — A PRECIOUS JEWEL

Looking unto Jesus the author and finisher of our faith....

Hebrews 12:2a

❧❧❧

I want to pay tribute to my mother, who went to be with the Lord during the Christmas holidays in 1993. My reason for doing this is two-fold. First, she is worthy of tribute for her service to the Lord and her family; and second, maybe I can help someone walk with the joy of the Lord through a similar situation in their life.

My mother was indeed a precious jewel. In fact, her name was Jewel! She was a blessing to everyone with whom she came in contact. If she had an enemy in this world, I do not know it. If she even thought someone was mad at her, she would make it right. Mother was loved by everyone who knew her. Since her death, I have received many cards and letters from people telling me how much she meant to them.

She had been the prayer coordinator for our ministry from its inception. The truth is, she kept us all in line long before we went into the ministry! She helped pray Happy into the kingdom of God, and was standing beside him laughing with joy when he received the baptism in the Holy Spirit. Every written or phoned-in prayer request was sent to her. She prayed for hours every day for the needs of people, an intercessor who loved praying. Many of the letters were streaked with her tears, because she truly loved people. Her intercession for Happy and me, as well as the body of Christ, will be greatly missed. Her prayers were effectual and fervent, full of love and power.

My mother was my best supporter. She was always there to cheer me on. When I first started my television show, I was so nervous and felt so inadequate. But she called me immediately after the show, just raving about how wonderful it was. I really thought it wasn't, but she thought it was and made me feel good about it!

On the other hand, Mother was also my best critic. She was bluntly honest. I could depend on her to tell me the truth about anything and that was good, because so many people won't tell you the truth. They are afraid they will offend you. But she could get away with it, because she was my mother!

Mother was my dearest friend, my shopping buddy, someone with whom I could share my hopes and dreams. I could always depend on her. I have three sisters, and each of us had a unique relationship with her. She was not partial to any of us. We were her girls. All of us at different times had written her poems, sharing how much she meant to us. She had them framed and hung them along the hallway in her home.

On December 1, 1993, I taped two of my sisters and mother on my television program, which would air the week of Christmas. We sang Christmas songs and talked about Christmas memories from years past. Mother told me afterwards that she did not want to do the program at all, but that it was something we girls would always have in case something ever happened to her. Well, she didn't even get to see the show. She had a massive heart attack on Saturday, December 11, and went to be with the Lord after bypass surgery on Friday, December 17. Her heart had been so damaged from the heart attack that it could not heal itself. She never regained consciousness after the surgery.

This was quite a shock to us. Mother and I had been shopping the day she had the heart attack, and we didn't even know she had heart problems. She was so full of energy and looked much younger than her years. She turned seventy-five the morning she died, and the doctors said, "It was a miracle she lived through the heart attack." They felt it was because she had a young body.

Each one of us have had to walk through this kind of adversity, and I am happy to say that God has indeed been our "tower of strength." I have always known the Word was alive, but I never realized just how much until the Word walked me through this sorrowful time — without sorrow.

I was dreading the memorial service. So, I put on a Stephen B. Stevens tape called, "Freedom from Oppression." I listened to the Word over and over the whole time I was getting dressed. I walked into my living room and put on Kenneth Copeland's "London Praise" tape and worshiped the Lord along with him. I walked the room praising God. I felt His presence.

At one time, I looked up and said with anger, "I hate death." God spoke right back and said, "I do too. It is my enemy." It shocked me, even though I knew that was true. Death is the last enemy to be put under Jesus' feet. How God helped me! I saw we were in this thing together and He was there to see me through it. He had walked through it before, and He was going to walk me through with His strength, which was His joy.

The Bible says in 1 Thessalonians 4:13b, **. . . that ye sorrow not, even as others which have no hope.** We have hope and believe in the resurrection, so we are commanded not to sorrow. Isaiah 53:4a says, **Surely he hath borne our griefs, and carried our sorrows.** Because he has paid the price, we don't have to bear grief and sorrow. We give them to Him. We cast all our cares over on Him, because He cares for us. (1 Pet. 5:7.)

I am not saying that this is easy! But I am saying that it works, if you apply His Word to your particular situation. Do not let the devil keep you from enjoying your life on this earth and doing what you are called to do. Cast your sorrow and grief over on Him. You can trust Him, because He is faithful and His Word is alive. The Word actually felt tangible during my time of sorrow. Quite frankly, it has stayed with me ever since.

In January of 1994 while on vacation, holy anger rose up in me against the devil. I began to speak out loud, out of my mouth, of my hatred for him. I realized it was coming from my spirit, so I started writing it down as it came out of my mouth. In essence, I told the devil that I hated him with a passion, that I was furious, fighting mad, and that I was going to destroy his works on this earth to the very best of my ability. I told him I was going to spoil his house in every way. By the authority I have in the Name of Jesus, I was going to heal the sick, cast out demons, and raise the dead.

The Lord showed me later that this is exactly what He did when John the Baptist was beheaded. He went into the wilderness (and I believe He felt the hurt that I felt), but He came out of the wilderness healing the sick, casting out demons, and raising the dead. Therefore, I declare and decree that I am going to do more for Jesus than I have ever done before!

Chapter Thirty-Two

WHO WILL PRAY?

The Lord will perfect that which concerneth me: thy mercy, O Lord, endureth for ever.

Psalm 138:8a

One of the things that concerned me most after the homegoing of my precious mother was *who* the prayer coordinator for our ministry would be. She had prayed for our ministry since its inception and prayed fervently for all those who called or sent in prayer requests.

I read the letters people sent, many describing desperate situations, and my heart would break. I said to my secretary, "Who is going to pray for these precious people?" I said to Happy, "Who in the world will take mother's place in interceding for the people?" It concerned me greatly.

Now don't misunderstand me. We have a lot of powerful intercessors at Agape Church. In fact, our church was founded on intercessory prayer. We pray every Sunday, Monday, and Wednesday nights. Each Tuesday at noon all our ministers fast and pray, and our staff prays together every weekday morning. But I knew how my mother took such a *personal* interest in the needs of the people and she prayed passionately for them. It was her life and calling.

Well, I have learned something. When a person is concerned about a situation or thing and there is a real burden, it is a good indication that the Holy Spirit is moving *that person* to do the job. I heard an evangelist say one time that a man came up to him after a big crusade where hundreds of people were saved and said, "You evangelists come into town and all these people get saved, then you leave. Who is going to follow up with them?" He said this because he thought the evangelist should. The evangelist answered very wisely, "I am not going to be caught doing what God has called *you* to do." There was one time when I would not have understood that remark. But I sure do now!

A few months after mother's death, while the ministers and I were praying, all of a sudden the Holy Spirit came upon me like a cloak. He said to me, "You have been asking Me who is going to take the position your mother had as an intercessor. I want you *to receive the mantle that she had.*" I told Him I would, and for the next thirty minutes I wept uncontrollably. I felt as if I was wrapped in a blanket of love and compassion. I cried until all my makeup was gone. The ministry staff knew something was happening in me. I told them afterwards what had happened and they laid hands on me and prayed. From that day forward, I have been diligently praying for the needs of the people. I am now an intercessor.

You might be thinking, "That's no big deal. You are in the ministry and you should be praying." I did pray, but the responsibility of being an intercessor for the ministry was an awesome one and something *I did not want.* I had said many times that I was not an intercessor and did not want to become one. It was not my gift or calling. I have learned to be careful with what I say!

I now find it quite a joy to pray for the needs of others. My spirit is so excited about it that when I wake up in the morning I hear "tongues" rolling around inside, ready to give birth to something in the earth. It is really exciting.

I am reminded of the story I heard T. L. Osborn tell about the time when the great Evangelist Charles Price went to be with the Lord. Brother Osborn said he went into the woods and wept, crying, "Oh God, who is going to take his place?" The Lord replied, "You are."

If you have been asking God to do a particular thing through someone else, you better be ready, because *you* might be called to do the job yourself!

Chapter Thirty-Three

HOLD FAST TO YOUR DREAMS

I will instruct thee and teach thee in the way which thou shalt go: I will guide thee with mine eye.

Psalm 32:8

We recognize our high school graduates by giving them a banquet after church. Each family is present with their son or daughter, and it is a beautiful event. On one occasion, Happy shared some thoughts with them about his high school days.

He really had not known what he wanted to do with his life, so he went to college, then into the Navy. Later he went to work, still not knowing exactly what to do with his life — until he was born again. Then God called him into the ministry. God had plans for him all along, but Happy had to get saved before he could receive them.

As Happy was talking, I began to think back to my high school days. Like the graduates we were honoring that day, I had had to make some decisions about my life. It can be very difficult for young people at that time of their life. However, I was born again and, as I said earlier in this book, felt strongly that I would like to be a pastor's wife. I told my best girlfriend, and she thought I had lost my mind! Her mother was the secretary at the church we attended and said to me, "You have no idea the stuff a pastor has to go through. You sure do not want that." Therefore, I did not talk about it anymore.

A few months later a young, unmarried man became pastor of a church down the street from where I lived. I decided to visit his church. Actually, I was thinking to myself, "This might be the pastor I am supposed to marry." But my pastor came to see me right away to let me know I was making a big mistake leaving my home church. He said I needed to come back. Having confidence in him, I returned. Eventually, the desire to marry a preacher just left me. No one thought I knew what I wanted, and I sure did not know what to do, so I pushed it out of my mind.

After graduation, it seemed the devil did everything he could to totally destroy my life and my witness for Jesus. I was a mixed-up young girl, not really knowing where to turn. I did not have fellowship with the Lord. I was not baptized in the Holy Ghost, and I did not know the Word. As a result, I just made one mistake after another.

The devil knew I had a call on my life, because I had dedicated my life to God for "special service" when I was fifteen years old. Satan was out to stop me, though. But do you know what? Satan is a loser. I married Happy thinking he was a Christian. And how I rejoiced later when he was actually born again! Then God called us into the full-time ministry. Glory to Him!

The funny thing is, I had totally forgotten that when I was a young teenager I had wanted to marry a preacher. It was my sweet Lord Who spoke to my heart the day Happy was ordained into the ministry, reminding me, "Jeanne, you are the wife of a preacher. You now have the desire of your heart." I was so overwhelmed with joy and deliriously thrilled in my heart. I felt joy unspeakable and full of glory. Once again, God proved Himself faithful to His call upon my life.

If you have an unction, a stirring deep in your heart about what you desire to be, *hold fast to your dream.* Don't let anyone steal it from you. More than likely, it is the Spirit of the Almighty God wanting to lead, guide, and direct you into exactly what He has for you to do. Run your race with patience, letting Him guide you with His gentle, never-failing hand.

Chapter Thirty-Four

BAPTIZED UNTO HIM

And Jesus, when he was baptized, went up straightway out of the water: and, lo, the heavens were opened unto him, and he saw the Spirit of God descending like a dove, and lighting upon him.

And lo a voice from heaven, saying, This is my beloved Son, in whom I am well pleased.

Matthew 3:16-17

For a period of six years in the eighties, Happy and I went to Jerusalem, Israel, with Dr. Lester Sumrall. We co-hosted the International Leadership Conference Tours. Every year ministers from other nations joined us along with large numbers of people. It was an exciting time, and I never got tired of going. As a matter of fact, it was the highlight of our year.

We visited all the historical and biblical places. We walked where Jesus and other great men of faith walked. We saw where Jesus was born and raised and where He died and was buried. It was wonderful to be in the presence of His empty tomb. On a plaque above the Garden Tomb is written, "He is not here. He is risen." Hallelujah!

We also went to the Jordan River where Jesus was baptized by

John the Baptist. Each year people wanted to get baptized where Jesus was baptized. I will have to admit, to my shame, that I thought these people were spiritually immature.

On the third day of one tour, the tour guide told us what our activities for the next day would be. We were to visit the Jordan River. He said, "If any of you want to be baptized, please bring a change of clothes." At that very moment, the Spirit of the Lord said to me, "Jeanne, I want you to be baptized." I was shocked beyond words. I said, "But Lord, I have already been baptized. Do You want me to be baptized again?" He never answered me. In fact, He never said another word. He had told me what to do and it was up to me to obey or disobey.

I did not mention this to anyone, not even my husband. I just pondered it in my heart. The next morning, I packed a little bag with a change of clothes in it. Happy said, "What are you doing?" I said, "The Lord wants me to be baptized." Happy never said another word either. He knew the way I felt about this, so he knew the Lord had spoken to me. Happy was the minister in charge of our bus, so he was the one doing the baptizing, which was an added blessing to me.

I still remember how icy cold the Jordan River was when I stepped into it. However, I had such a great expectancy about what was going to happen that I did not care. When it was my turn to be baptized, I walked out where Happy was and he baptized me. I cannot express what the cool water on my face felt like as I was coming out of the water. It was an awesome sensation. I felt the Lord's presence upon me and around me.

I do not understand the significance of it all myself, but I do understand that Jesus was not pleased with my judgmental thoughts about His children wanting to be baptized where He was baptized.

He knew my attitude needed to be adjusted. It definitely has been and I am thankful for it!

If we will humble ourselves in the sight of the Lord, He will lift us up. He will cleanse us from all unrighteousness and put a *right* spirit within us. That is how He perfects us in His love. If we will let Him, He will clean us up!

That night when I went to sleep, I had a beautiful dream. I saw myself laying hands on people and miraculous healings were taking place. When I awoke, the words of the song "Baruch, Hashem, Adonai" kept going over and over in my mind. *Baruch* means blessed, *Hashem* means name or reputation, and *Adonai* means Lord. The title of this song in English is, "Blessed Be the Name of the Lord."

I had been baptized where Jesus was baptized, and the reality of being baptized in His name struck me with awe. I thought of all the wonderful blessings for us in His names:

Jehovah-Rohi:	The Lord is my shepherd
Jehovah-Shalom:	The Lord is my peace
Jehovah-Ropheka:	The Lord is my health
Jehovah-Tsidkenu:	The Lord is my righteousness
Jehovah-Shammah:	The Lord is my companion
Jehovah-Nissi:	The Lord is my victory
Jehovah-Jirah:	The Lord is my provision

Praise the Name of the Lord!

Jeanne Caldwell is co-founder of Agape Church in Little Rock, Arkansas, with her husband, Happy Caldwell. She is an ordained minister, anointed by the Holy Spirit as a teacher and singer.

Jeanne hosts a weekly television program called, "In His Presence" on their Christian television stations, KVTN-25 in Little Rock, and KVTH-26 in Hot Springs, Arkansas. She conducts a monthly Ladies Bible Study for the ladies of Agape Church and surrounding cities. She also hosts a powerful Ladies Fall seminar each year where women attend from all over the United States. She has recorded 12 record albums; 10 with her husband, Happy, and their son, Ronnie, known as "The Agape Singers," and two solo albums called, "The Peaceable Kingdom" and "Jeanne."

Ministering the Word of God with boldness and clarity, Jeanne's inspiring messages and anointed songs have blessed and healed many. Because God has given her a heart for ministering to His people, she shares with authority and personal experience how to defeat the devil in every area of life. She can understand their need and encourage them to boldly pursue God for the answers...for He is faithful!

In Canada, contact:

Word Alive
P.O. Box 670
Niverville, Manitoba
Canada R0A 1E0

The Harrison House Vision

Proclaiming the truth and the power
Of the Gospel of Jesus Christ
With excellence;

Challenging Christians to
Live victoriously,
Grow spiritually,
Know God intimately.